The FABULOUS EKPHRASTIC FANTASTIC ESSAYS

The Fabulous Ekphrastic Fantastic!

Copyright © 2020 by Miah Jeffra

Interior design by Aidan Forster
Cover design by Seth Pennington

Author photo: Sean Mikula

Interior photos courtesy of the author.

Sibling Rivalry Press, LLC
PO Box 26147
Little Rock, AR 72221

info@siblingrivalrypress.com

www.siblingrivalrypress.com

ISBN: 978-1-943977-73-4

Library of Congress Control No. 2019953146

By special invitation, this title is housed in the Rare Book and Special Collections Vault of the Library of Congress.

First Sibling Rivalry Press Edition, March 2020

The FABULOUS EKPHRASTIC FANTASTIC

ESSAYS

MIAH JEFFRA

SIBLING RIVALRY PRESS
DISTURB/ENRAPTURE
LITTLE ROCK, ARKANSAS

CONTENTS

"I like to pretend that my art has nothing to do with me."

– Roy Lichtenstein

IF THE DAY EVER COMES

(after David Wojnarowicz's
Untitled (One Day This Kid))

ONE DAY THIS KID will take photographs to make still, a life. One day this kid will still their life, as if waiting to become one. One day this kid will think they're a girl, then think he's a boy, will grow a beard, will dye their eyelashes, but ultimately will harden their feet and walk barefoot. One day this kid will often be wrong, most often when they are certain. One day this kid will exist on both sides of a boundary. One day this kid will say to their heartbroken friends that   in order to love beyond fiction, you must break a heart and   have your heart broken. One day this kid will   look at scars like buddhas. One day this   kid will move to Los Angeles and hate it,   until they love it. One day this kid will be-   come too political, and then realize their   ambiguity is far more useful. One day this   kid will find the ambiguous a buddha.   One day this kid will play top, bottom and   sideways. One day this kid realizes that shapes   without right angles fit into edges with room to   spare. One day this kid will learn to use   edges sparingly. One day   this kid will apprehend   the danger of lan-   guage, and

11

wield it. One day the wielding will edge the boundaries with a glint of blade, and the kid won't know whose flesh is flayed. One day this kid will hug close that fear is the opposite of love. One day this kid will be accused of a hug-load of fear. One day this kid will have to admit this to be true. One day this kid will not be afraid to hurt. One day this kid won't remember one home. One day this kid will understand why their mother made a new one. One day this kid will learn how to make a home out of one material. One day this kid will look at themselves and hate it, until they love it. One day this kid will sing and dance out loud in public, because they want to be the last faggot on earth to give a fuck. One day this kid will realize the world hasn't changed that much. One day this kid will wonder if choosing what to remember is a kind of lie. One day this kid will quit tangling love with memory. One day this kid will love with one material. One day this kid will finally fuck without shame. One day this kid will take a long time. One day this kid will know confusion and fury, and look at their brother with apology. One day this kid will stop apologizing. One day this kid will forgive their father, because they discover who forgiveness is for. One day this kid will stop being so damned serious. One day this kid will realize that comedy is just activism with some sugar on the tip. One day this kid will become a strong ass mother-fucker. One day this kid will realize they always were. One day this kid will learn not to hold on too tight. One day this kid will do something right for a change. One day this kid will never stop dancing. One day the stitching will be cut away from this kid's lips, but will they say enough that matters?

TO AN EX-LOVER

(after *A Natural History of the Senses*)

WHEN I WAS SIXTEEN, I saw an alien. True story. My mama and I were watching television in our narrow low-rent Baltimore rowhouse when we heard our dog barking with a particular urgency. Mama asked me to go investigate. I walked to the back, flipped the floodlight switch and opened the door. And there, at the end of our narrow concrete sliver of a yard, was Eggroll, looking up at a chest-high figure with an oblong luminescent face and large black eyes, staring directly at my smaller-than-average, teenage, presently and keenly vulnerable self. And immediately, without even a flash of hesitation, I shit my pants; a small, yet substantial, perfectly compacted brown nugget bulleted from my buttcheeks like a backfired slingshot. I could feel the velocity of that single turd shoot against the lining of my poly-cotton Voltron pajama bottoms, the betrayal of years of self-control, the pastel illustrations of *Once Upon a Potty* flashing into my mind's eye, as I waddled back to my mother with a face whiter than Ann Coulter. Ann Coulter. Wearing an eggshell bikini. On a foggy day. In a salt mine.

Vision is a tricky enterprise. All we truly perceive are configurations of shadows and light. True story. 127 million photoreceptors detect light stimulus, a chemical, then become electrical impulse along the optic nerve to the brain, the mind, an open file without a name. And from this, we begin to make sense of our world.

My niece at nine months, beginning to crawl. One day I watched her amble directly into a piece of furniture, head-first. She thrusted with determined hands and knees, without hesitation, right into my sister's backless Wayfair barstool. Did little Mackenzie not see the metal legs? Why did she careen right into that pain, the boo-boo on her forehead? It appeared as if she hadn't seen the stool at all. *Shadows and light, chemical, electrical impulse, an open file.* And then, my sister, *Mommy* to the rescue: She said, "Chair." Baby stare. "Chair." Baby stare. "Chair." Baby stare. Now, the open file *has* a name: language, a label, the sign.

Neurolinguist Richard Gregory argues that seeing is entirely hypothesis, reliant on experience and memory. We encounter a particular configuration of shadows and light, and that configuration is then matched to the closest file we have in our database. Your brain is a file clerk, searching for the match. That closest match is then pulled up and projected onto our mind's silver-screen. And that is what we see—not what we *perceive*, but what we see. Everyone knows a filing system is unsuccessful without explicit labeling. Labels are language. In essence, language becomes more our eyes than our eyes.

Do you know the story of the Aztec genocide? The great, advanced civilization that initially and fatally opened its arms to Cortes' swords? They had a myth: The god of rebirth, Quetzalcoatl, promised to return one day from the East on a bed of clouds to bestow upon the Aztecs the fortunes, the white hot heart of the morning star. And then one day, in the dead middle of a millennium, upon the horizon, fishermen saw what they believed to be, approaching from the East, in billowing white, the promises of that morning star. See, the Aztecs were not sea-farers. And the billowing sails of Cortes' ships, well, the Aztecs didn't have a file for that, and those sails wound up becoming a different kind of promise.

And this is how you perceived me: a promise, a myth. I wonder what the story was that begat your creation of me. But I was not seen, that is certain; you were searching for a match. The language of the story you knew before you never knew me projected onto your mind's silver screen before I even approached. And the Hollywood dream you thought you saw was all light and shadow along the walls of a cave. And so you opened your heart, as if you hadn't even seen that I was only strong enough to conquer—not love—and you careened right into that pain. I am sorry for that.

If you haven't figured it out yet, I didn't really see an alien. I saw a possum on our back fence. The floodlight wasn't strong enough to pick up the chain-link at all, but it could reflect the rodent's iridescent fur on the top of its head, pointed down to keep a watchful eye on the threatening stance of my vicious Shih Tzu mix. The pose in illumination suggested the shape of that most common of mediated aliens—the bulbous head and sunken long face. My hypothesis was dead wrong. I didn't have a file in my database for something as odd as a possum on a fence in an inner-city Baltimore neighborhood. And, of course, what were my mama and I watching in the living room before the encounter? Mulder and Scully, forever engrossed in their sexually frustrated tête-à-têtes between science and magic. But in my mind's eye, in my memory, I still see that four-foot alien staring directly into my being as clear now as it was then, crystal enough to make me drop a stink pickle in my drawers.

When you don't collect much data, you don't have much in your database.

Recently, after watching a performance on YouTube, Ann Coulter called out Beyoncé for her salacious, female-demeaning lyrics as an ironic parallel to the accusations of Trump's equally recent gender blitz. Ann tweets: "Beyoncé, cited by Michelle Obama as role model for her daughters, sings about 'pussy curvalicious, served delicious.' Oh my. I just fainted." End tweet. Ann was probably promenading victorious at this burn, this apparent demonstrated hypocrisy of the smug liberal elite. However, what Ann didn't realize during that cock-sure strut in her proverbial pencil skirt was that the woman she perceived mouthing those lyrics was not Beyoncé at all, but Nicki Minaj. Supporters defended Ann's mistake by saying, "They look so much alike."

Black woman. Beyoncé. Black woman. Beyoncé. Black woman...

When you don't collect much data, you don't have much in your database.

This tells me how we perceive one another: educated guesses, inaccurate file names, projected images, subservient to language. This tells me that if you were to see me clearly, you would have had to learn my language. Or, to learn a language beyond your own. Beyond the language of myth, and even beyond the language of billowing sails. This tells me that we all need to learn as much language as we can to quit running into things that are there that we can't see. This tells me that if we commit to this—you and I, all of us—maybe then we will finally escape the shadows of the cave.

OTHERWISE

(after Joan Brown's *Noel in the Kitchen*)

YOU CAN ONLY SEE A CHILDHOOD when you pull as far back as the years of it. Otherwise, it is all feeling: the texture of a dog's fur, the fine grain of checkered linoleum, butter on a plate, a chip in the Formica.

Time provides a frame, borders nailed into right angles, suitable for hanging.

A story. A photograph. Clear lines making memories with beginnings and ends. Enter mother, exit brother. Enter father, exit the bedroom door. Frames. Angles. A different vantage.

The more you stare at something, the more its shapes flatten with the background.

I'm sure my father had a texture. His hands would scoop me by my armpits and up onto his motorcycle. His coffee-laden tongue would lick my nose. His breath grazed my face when he laughed silly in front of the barbecue. He must be holding me to be so close to his breath. But I feel none of these things. I just can't feel them.

The more you stare at something, the less real it seems to be.

The weight of a window. The impossibility of a TV. Marbles on the carpet, and I wonder where my brother has run off to now. I wonder if he's running, even as he sleeps. I would reach out to touch him, but I'm afraid I wouldn't feel the thing. I'm afraid my fingers would slide right through.

A bedroom. A closet full of records. My older sister hides underneath the sheets, behind her hair, hides. I could brush the hair from her face, and perhaps, just perhaps, I would see what it looks like. A viscera. The bottom of memory, particles that can float. Watch how they dance in the light coming through the blinds. They glint but never graze the palm of my hand.

The more you stare at something, the more you feel it was never there.

The lightness of a door. The probability of a radio. The corners of a house bleed into blur, and my mother is the only thing with a clear line, in fine grain. The center of the frame. The years of it. Her ice blue eyes, a vantage I will always wonder. So much feeling. Otherwise, a childhood.

A kitchen. A water-stained counter. A sleeping dog lying on linoleum. I could place a marble on the floor by the stove, and it would roll steady to the back door. A long line. The bottom of a frame. A story. A photograph. This one tells me I'm allowed to feel exactly one thing. What would I choose? Is that a choice any of us can make?

DENOTATION/CONNOTATION
(OR, THE RELATIVITY OF SHIT)

(after Chris Ofili's *Holy Virgin Mary*)

LIKE ANY QUEER ARTIST of a certain age and disposition, I lost myself in the Brooklyn Museum of Art. In the last months of the Millennium, a fresh thing with gesso smeared on my pantlegs, Top Ramen broth staining my fingers. I was looking for something bold, beyond the exhausted sigh, beyond the high shoulders of the Y2K craze, looking for sensation. I forgot what it was.

And there she stood. An ink blot of a limbless figure, roll-of-the-dice eyes, a minstrel mouth, glossy cutouts of female genitalia as if caught in a butterfly net, a blob of elephant shit gooped on her left tit, the iconic blue shawl and spray of yellow around her head the viewer's only teddy bear.

Janey, my play-mate, my art-mate, an every kind of checkmate, whispered in my ear, "That's the most beautiful virgin I've ever seen." I smiled to her without turning my head. Like any queer artist of a certain age and disposition, we were stoned. And so proud of our ability to observe.

Give me the word that comes to mind when you think of a museum.

I was running from someone at the end of the Millennium. I was lost in the Brooklyn Museum of Art because it was big and it was full of things I had no control over. Janey sported overalls with metallic ribbons shooting from her pockets. We danced to the colors of the room, or we stared when the movement became too much touch for becoming.

Chris Ofili inspired the ire of pasta-sounding Catholics with this virgin, and particularly that of New York's most notorious, Rudy Giuliani. NEA 4 Rudy. Jesse Helms Rudy. Ruined New York with a sweep of his wrangled hand Rudy. *Time*'s Man of the Year not soon after, when a violence once again allowed folks to forget all the violence that came before.

For whatever reason, it wasn't the porn-mag pussies nor the black-faced Mary that made Rudy mad. It was the poop. Rudy said, "You can't do things that desecrate the most personal and deeply held views of people in society." Neoliberal Park Slope white folks loped in defense of Ofili, claimed that the artist was of Nigerian descent, and how in African culture elephant dung connotes power and fertility.

Ofili, born and raised in London, only said this about his work: "My Mary is simply a hip-hop version." Me, born and raised in hip-hop Baltimore, only said this about his work: "Can an entire continent be whittled to a single culture?"

Give me the word that comes to mind when you think of a museum.

That same year red-headed, spindle-limbed Craig Brown walked into his high school sporting a white t-shirt with a black swastika and the word RECLAIM in red stretched across his chest. Teachers pulled him out of homeroom rocking eyes the size of dinner plates. He pleaded that the symbol only recently bared sharp teeth, wickedness and war obliterating its spiritual connotation. That for histories before, its angles and lines leaned soft in the mouth and whispered: "What is in existence, will continue to exist."

Connotation: the socio-cultural and "personal" associations of a signifier, typically related to the viewer's class, age, gender, ethnicity and so on.

Denotation: what all viewers from any culture and at any time would recognize the signifier as signifying.

In other words, "We know the difference between the font of 20% more and the font of teriyaki," but they are merely fonts, shapes and gestures. And yet, our lips are wet with them.

I was running from someone at the end of the Millennium. I was lost in the Brooklyn Museum of Art because it was complicated and required nothing of me. I didn't read the didactics on the white wall. I only looked at the pictures and mimicked their shapes with my tongue.

When I said, "I need to be creative," he heard, "I need the space to create."

When he said, "You can have whatever you want," I heard, "As long as you color between my lines."

Give me the word that comes to mind when you think of a museum.

Chris Ofili became famous. He won the Turner Prize. And for the celebratory exhibition in the Tate Gallery, he installed a burlap bag filled with cow manure and placed it on a white pedestal. He called it *Bag of Shit*. Days after the exhibition opened, an unidentified figure towed a wheelbarrow full of cow manure up to the steps of the Tate Gallery and dumped it square in front of the entrance doors.

When Ofili said, "Modern art is full of shit," maybe the wheelbarrow man heard, "You can have whatever you want."

And when the wheelbarrow man said, "Modern art is full of shit," maybe Ofili heard, "Unless you color between my lines."

I was running from someone at the end of the Millennium. I was lost in the Brooklyn Museum of Art because I knew he wouldn't find me. But he was there.

Denotation: What is there. What is actually there.

Connotation: How our feelings spill into the lines of us all.

What is in existence will continue to exist.

Janey pulled a ribbon from her overalls and handed it to me. She said, "This is your offering to the virgin." I asked her, "But where shall I place it?" I've never been able to answer that question. She took my arm in hers, and that sensation: the closest I would ever be to belonging. A fresh thing. A word that comes to mind. But I already forgot what it was.

LATITUDES

THAT FIST. Despite the silliness of my mother's emoji-tongue, the look-how-crazy-I-am face, the candid delight of her expression, her fist is what grabs me. It isn't the surprise of it, but the familiarity. That hand doesn't guide the steering wheel, it clutches the thing, begs it to never leave. I can imagine the flesh impressed white from that need to hold on. And all the while, you can see her leaning towards me. I, the photographer, the one who renders still, a life.

This photo will never be posted—Mama would kill me—but it remains on the scrolling litany of my phone's stored memories, this one of the roadtrip we took summer 2017 through Alabama. We are crossing a bridge. She wanted to find places to move, worn and chapped by the Baltimore winters, the gunshots in the early mornings, being reminded of all that had already been lost. She wanted the sun, the simplicity, the South. She wanted the water—a lake, a river, a garden hose, no matter. She loves to stare out at water, viewing changeability from a safe distance. And so, we drove all around the state.

The sun is beginning to peek behind tall things, and the Southern light has cooled to the color of a peeled onion. Lightning bugs will soon beg with their horny blinking, and everything is in that still state between punching the clock and supper, made even more still by the weight of summer air in the river delta. If my uncle were waiting for us in a motel room—which he is not—he would be opening his third Coors Light and thinking about his five estranged children—one in prison for greed, one in prison for fury—hoping my mother returns soon to busy him out of

his regrets with weather talk and dinner plans.

Before we crossed this bridge, before I cranked up the volume to Right Said Fred's "I'm Too Sexy" on the only radio station that didn't blare post-9/11 Country or Christian Rock, I asked Mama if she resented that I had moved away, so far away. Her hands slid up the steering wheel as if she were a pre-teen hugging the neck of her middle school crush at a gymnasium dance. She looked forward into more than the horizon, and muttered, "Uh-uh." She couldn't sound out a word at that moment. The syllables would have given her away. I probably pretended not to see her tight lips, maybe even looked out the passenger window just long enough to see the alligators sunbathing on the side of the road, and shot through the silence with a "Look, Mama!" that reminded me of every day of my childhood.

In the motel room the night before with its burnt orange bedspreads, I poured her a glass of the only decent Pinot Noir they had at the Piggly Wiggly ("I swear Mama, they don't all taste like vinegar."). She asked me after a few sips—and the roses already blooming on her cheeks—why I had enjoyed so much success with love while she always failed. She twisted a tendril of her hair, and it made her seem younger somehow. I nodded my head back as if I had never thought of this question before (but I had many, many times). With a face as flummoxed as I could manage without her seeing through the bullshit (which she had many, many times), I said, "I learned from you." Which was almost true. I didn't say, "I learned what not to trust." I didn't say, "I learned how not to hold on too tight." I didn't say, "I learned to love myself first, before any other man." Even though often that man, for her, was me.

I live in San Francisco. Mama lives in Baltimore. If you held a ruler up to these two points on a map, you'd draw the longest straight line across America, yet one that rested precisely on the same latitude.

Before the motel room, before the sky reveals itself, before the crossing of another bridge, I photograph my mother, because I want to know if the pain I see in her living can be glimpsed in that still life. I want to know if anyone else can see it. When you love something so much, you see your own truths mapped over theirs, and the contours don't often align. A humid horizon. A changeable view. Sometimes, we need distance to see a thing clearly. Sometimes, clarity can be as closed as a fist. I don't know which truth this photograph demands, but for me, the demand is always beginning.

JUST ONE DAY OUT OF LIFE

(after Madonna's "Holiday")

MADONNA'S FIRST MAINSTREAM HIT SINGLE in the U.S. was "Holiday." It was released in 1983 and entered the Billboard Top 20 the week before Christmas. In the corresponding one-take video, Madonna, dressed in a black mesh top and scrunched hair, dances in the center with two other New Wavers—a joyful and gyrating routine signature of early 80s Danceteria New York. My mother said the video was "kind of trashy," but she thought the song was catchy and fun. I thought—my already seven-year-old budding obsession with Bowie, Prince and all things punk-lite—it was *rad*. And when Mama would say, "Let's clean house," we would bounce around, her singing into the feather duster and I promenading with our kitchen mop to the candy-pop rhythm.

Madonna recorded the song with her producer, Jellybean Benitez. I didn't much like jelly beans. But they were all the rage in Reagan-era America. I preferred butterscotch, which is why I was excited for Aikahi Elementary School's visit from Santa Claus the week before Christmas. The flyer for the assembly announced, "Santa will pass out butterscotch candies from his bag of gifts—if you're good!" We didn't eat much candy in my house on the Kane'ohe Bay Marine Corps base—my mother had been an assistant at a dental clinic and was dedicated to ensuring my older brother and I had immaculate teeth.

Aikahi loosely means "Steady Place" in Hawaiian. And it truly was. I loved school. Even though I was a shy child who didn't raise their hand, I could leave the chaos and anger of my home and learn to sing "Musunde

Hiraite," could watch poorly animated videos on solar systems beyond our own and could read about the Big Island volcano, Kilauea, that had erupted on my sixth birthday. I could go to school and listen to stories of how the Islands formed instead of my ill-equipped father and ADHD brother screaming at one another beyond my bedroom door.

Butterscotch was first known to be sold at Parkinson's of Doncaster in the mid-nineteenth century and was popularized by Queen Victoria herself when she sampled the confectionary. Its name derives from the combination of boiled butter and sugar, after which the concoction is "scotched," or cut into pieces, before hardening.

I was in the first row during the assembly, one of few advantages for being the shortest boy in class, and when Santa emerged from behind the scrim and sat down, I could almost touch him. He was fat and white-bearded, as one would expect. His "Ho" echoed as loudly here as in any suburban shopping mall rotunda. But there was something off about Santa this day. The white trim of his suit was dingy, and his cheeks blanch instead of blush. When he sat down in his chair, he sighed heavy and rubbed his temples.

He signaled our teachers to pass out the candy while he proclaimed that toy production in the North Pole was booming, and Mrs. Claus says hello, and how good so many of us had been this year. As I popped the creamy butterscotch in my mouth, I wondered if he knew I had been bad—oh, my *thoughts*. That last week I imagined cutting out my father's tongue. I was tired of hearing him yell at my mother across dinner tables and couches, screaming at her things I only heard in the movies my brother snuck on TV. When he would storm out of the house, as he often did, I sometimes hoped he wouldn't return. My brother wailed and shouted at her as well, calling her trash—that word again—and I remember my mother calling Madonna that once, but I didn't quite understand. It was just so much *noise*. And then my mother, afterward, auburn hair falling around her face as she sat on the bed in her dark room. I wanted people to leave. I would soon be granted that wish, but not exactly how I had meant it.

I savored my butterscotch. I let it rest under my tongue and would only pull the sweetness when my salivary glands demanded. While other kids had sucked furiously to wear their butterscotch down to a yellow imprint on their tongue, or the even more impatient ones had bit into and chewed it up, I was steadfast. Mine was very much whole and round and delightful, even at the moment the teachers could see that most kids were getting restless. So, they began the sing-a-long, first to "Jingle Bells."

And this is when I really noticed how uncomfortable Santa was. As the room filled with screeching off-key yelps and cackled caroling of "Batman smells" and "Robin laid an egg," I watched Santa pat his forehead with the inside of his palm and slide his hand down to his planetoid belly like he was giving it reassurance. I thought Santa must be coming down with a cold or flu, which explained why I could smell something like cough syrup or hydrogen peroxide emanating from his body.

And that's when I saw it. While the assembly rocked in their chairs to a shouting, spirited rendition of "Rudolph the Red-Nosed Reindeer," Santa slowly tilted the left side of his body ever so slightly, and right at the "won't you guide my sleigh tonight?" he released a melisma of tone-descending farts that began as staccato raspberries and slowed and flattened with the resignation of a balloon that knows the hole won't ever close; ending with a tiny, almost imperceptible squeak, like Tinkerbell had exhaled her final breath. The look of relief on Santa was profound. He was a different man; happy again, jolly even. And *I* realized something at that moment, a sudden wisdom equally profound as Santa's relief: the eruption of Kilauea was mother earth farting.

One day we come together, to release the pressure.

I was so shocked that Santa had squeezed out such a musical display, that this otherworldy not-quite-real-human could even fart, so moved by the subsequent correlation I had made between the body and the world, that I forgot about the butterscotch stowed under my tongue, and in my reactive gasp, sucked it down my windpipe. And it went deep. I tried to cough but couldn't catch any air. I even raised my hands over my head like I had been taught in school, but I did so with too much oomph and sailed backwards out of my chair, which is when everyone stopped singing and looked over at the commotion. The next thing I know the butterscotch is stuck in the berber carpet a foot from my mouth, and Santa is looming over me, "Are you all right, kid?" Disoriented, but still clear enough in my eureka, I said to Santa, "Volcanoes are buttholes."

More than the trauma of being asphyxiated by my favorite candy, I was mortified that I, tiny and quiet Miah Jeffra, had cut the first-grade Christmas assembly to an early conclusion, one of the few events all kids looked forward to. I didn't dare to speak, from the muttered epiphany to Santa until I was safely in my bedroom. I knew I would suffer at the gathering cruelty of seven-year-old vocabulary those three long days before Christmas break. The torture would be real, and it would be heinous. I had compromised my only Aikahi. The class didn't even get to tell Santa what they wanted for Christmas. And maybe, just for that *only*, I was relieved, because I didn't know what I'd have told him.

When I finally summoned the courage to emerge from my room, there was my mother. I'm not sure where my father and brother were, but it was quiet, and I was grateful. She had the feather duster in one hand and the mop in the other, which she extended to me, and said, "Santa told me you were a pretty wise fella," and grinned. I flipped the mop over, so that the gray tendrils fell like dreadlocks around the flat-headed girl I had named Molly. My mother turned on the stereo, and we wiggled to Madonna's "Holiday," as we had done many a time, the feather duster her microphone, the upside-down mop my dancing partner. And, all was forgotten—the embarrassment, the chaos—at least for now.

Soon after the New Year, my mother would leave us and move in to a small apartment on the other side of Kane'ohe Bay. I guess she wanted the noise to stop, too. Mama knew that before we all hardened, she had to cut our family into pieces. But at that moment, all was forgotten.

Just one day out of life. It would be, it would be so nice.

DOWNHILL STUFF

THE CHILD IS FROZEN in mid-dance. He clutches the end of a threadbare *Jaws* t-shirt, wears gold lamé slippers. The boy next to him studies his brother, mimics the movement. Knees dropped, knees in. A shuffle. The older boy wears a t-shirt that says, "Here Comes the Incredible Hulk," and jeans. The room is brown and green. Brown carpet, brown armchair, brown hair, green eyes. Plants in the foreground. The little one is center, looks right at the camera, while the other is off to the side. Two brothers, at play.

The photo rests in a plastic sheath on a clear plastic Rolodex album. Instead of turning pages, one rotates a knob and the photos turn on a wheel, looping to reveal a new picture. There is no end and no beginning. There are several of this moment, this dance, this living room in Camp Pendleton, 1979. Mama has pulled out her guitar, and her boys yell over one another their requests. For Chris, Chuck Berry's "Johnny B Good." For me, John Denver's "Downhill Stuff." I assume position as Mama plays my song. My toddler body, a dance, an ekphrasis of its own. Her voice is rich and loamy. As a young child I confused it with Linda Ronstadt on the radio.

Some people like that downhill stuff
They like it fast and breezy
Some people walk on the other side
They like it slow and easy

Outside is a Southern California constant, only the veteran resident perceiving the difference in color between winter and spring, the thousand shades of California blue. The Inupiaq of Alaska have 70 words for ice. The brine of the Pacific, the hum of the Navy Hospital, are faint on the breeze. If my father were home—which he is not—he would be slipping a turkey pot pie into the microwave, slathering it with mustard, and slipping behind a wall, while Mama played and we danced. I have very few memories of my father at home. I'm sure there were fond moments, but I remember few.

Before the dancing, before I could insist on "Downhill Stuff" and work my meaty legs into ecstatic wobbling, before the joy of my mother's guitar, Chris attacked a plant, maybe even the plant in the foreground. One minute he sat on the couch, the next he was cleaving leaves. He screamed, "The snakes!" in wide-eyed horror. Mama wrestled him down, held him until his vision cleared. The delusion was triggered by a blood sugar drop. Onset juvenile diabetes. My mother sighed, another privation in the bind of motherhood. Chris was a hyperactive child, a fidgeting streak. He didn't want to be held, he didn't want to heed. Smart and strong, sweet as sugar one minute, another minute a hulk. My mother never stopped chasing him, and we were a family that ran. And this, a new hardship.

My mother was 17 when she gave birth to my brother. She was already presumed a woman, then a wife. The pregnancy triggered her to be kicked out of high school. The pregnancy also triggered metastatic thyroid cancer, a scar across her throat. And her husband, our father, walked out on her, "couldn't handle it," while she puked from chemo, another scar, this one raking across her youth. There is only so much a body can take. But my mother survived, and my mother took on being a mother, and my mother took my father back, who was willing once she had healed. And though he returned, he was hardly ever there. And, I wonder, too, about her healing.

Sometimes we work just to try to make a living
Or we're working just to make it pay
Sometimes we're trying to work our will
But that won't work anyway

My brother was 14 when my parents finally split for good, this time my mother doing the leaving. We were stationed in Kane'ohe Bay, Hawai'i. By then Chris was almost always a full-fledged hulk. Manic rages, ripping picture frames off walls, wielding his fists. My mother would try to calm him, and when he faced her, Chris would scream, "What is wrong with me?" through hot tears. By now, he had become too strong for my mother to hold him down until his vision cleared, and her exhaustion was thick as the bulging tendons in her neck. Before her entire youth was reduced to a map of scars, she took the only road she found legible. In the wake of her leaving, I retreated to my bed, would summon the comfort of Shenandoah, an imaginary older sister, from the shadows of my room. In the wake of her leaving, my brother spiraled further. He became a monster, and my father was ill-equipped—certainly strong enough to hold Chris down, but not strong enough to show his love for him. He did love my brother, this I know. I saw it in his exasperated sighs, his gritted teeth. But it takes strength to show love, and that was a muscle my father hadn't worked out. Soon after, he dropped us with my grandparents to live, while he found a new wife, a new life.

Three years later, after we had just moved back in with my mother, in a trailer park in Hanover, Maryland, my brother slipped into his first alcohol-induced coma on a stranger's front lawn. He was 17. When he came to, body strapped face-down on the gurney, his first words were complaint: that the paramedics cut through and ruined his jean jacket to resuscitate his body. At the same age my mother struggled to save her life, my brother was wasting his. I sometimes wonder if my father's absence is the main story between these bookends.

Oh everybody's looking for heaven
Everybody's looking for hope
Everybody looking for higher and higher
But nobody wants to be looking alone

But a life is more than its most harrowing stories, a traumatic life more than its traumatic chapters. I don't ever think of these memories as pages to turn, anyway. Within the tumult of my mother's motherhood, there is laughter, generosity and joy. There were road-trips in the conversion van, and picnics on the beach. I have memories of my brother goofy and I have memories of him kind. I have memories of my mother smiling and bright, often when music was playing on the reel-to-reel, or we were dancing with the mop and broom while cleaning house, or when she had her six-string Ovation in hand. These memories are no longer tethered to something as fixed as time. They loop around, as if on a wheel, no end or beginning.

My mother stopped playing her guitar soon after she lost her voice. Scar tissue from surgery grew in her throat well after the cancer was gone. Eventually, it pressed against her cords like a thumb to a guitar string. And then, yelling over idling dump-trucks at the recycling plant she worked at paralyzed what she had left. Whenever a friend or relative slips into nostalgia, and hark back to that soft earth of her voice, my mother's eyes dim for just a moment before she says something like, "Well, what are you going to do?"

Keep a moving in a forward direction
Like a river rolling down to the sea
If you want to make different selection
Honey let yourself go with gravity

I am dancing in gold lamé slippers. My brother mimics my movement. I look right at the camera, my brother off to the side. Two brothers. Two lives, rolling as they do, and gravity only guarantees one thing.

MY OWN FIRELIGHT
(after *My Own Private Idaho*)

IN THE CAMPFIRE SCENE of Gus Van Sant's *My Own Private Idaho*, River Phoenix's character, Mike, says to a slightly out of frame, out of focus Scott, played by Keanu Reeves, "I want to be close to you." Their faces glow that seductive orange, and the rest of the frame is dark, highlighting the intimacy that only a campfire can create. Mike continues, his eyes never leaving the firelight, "I mean, I know we're close, but I want to be closer." The sound of the two men's boots shifting on the ground, and Mike's struggle to express his love for Scott, is so tactile, so intimate, that my 16-year-old self may have forgotten to breathe. The scene ends with Scott inviting Mike into his arms to spoon through the night. The gesture is kind, gentle and sensitive. Not sexual, but certainly romantic.

The film is loosely based on Shakespeare's *Henry IV* and, in particular, the evolution of Prince Hal, who, like Scott, eschews his royal blood to cavort with the characters of a Caravaggio painting. There is a romance to that, certainly—lack is exotic fodder for one who has never felt it. And the indefinable role in a culture as subterranean as this may attract a man who has known the destiny of his whole life since birth. Perhaps Prince Hal was Shakespeare's "fair youth," the beautiful and reckless subject of so many sonnets, the ones that raise eyebrows and speculations over Shakespeare's nature even today.

Scott and Mike are both hustlers. Scott is straight, only has sex with men who pay him. Mike is attracted to women, as well, but has surprised himself with his feelings for Scott. So, is Mike bisexual? And if Scott truly is straight, why does he spoon with Mike, in this tender, romantic moment? Van Sant suggests that these questions matter little, as he never spends another moment attempting to clarify the relationship between these two friends. Instead, he allows their relationship to be, to breathe, to blur, throughout their rambling, ramshackle quest, from Oregon to Italy to Idaho, presumably to find Mike's long-lost mother.

I wanted it. The closeness of their friendship, their love, somewhere between brotherhood and romance. My face drew into the movie frame with a longing that would make a dog howl. Not for the sex, but for the intimacy. Maybe I could relate to Mike's quest, somehow, and thus, we shared the same need. This was a love that had no label, but I believed its truth lived in our human heart.

In high school, I almost had it with C. We would listen to REM's *Murmur* on the floor of my bedroom, and allow the shared solitude, the reflective lyrics, to render us whispered and vulnerable, a curtain pulled back, an armor that didn't need to be worn. But that spell would be broken all too quickly once the horde of our classmates made things again loud and jocular, and soon it became difficult for either one of us to return to that quietness. And then, it stopped happening altogether. Perhaps we were both unsure what that shared space meant. What I *was* sure about: it felt good. Mike and Scott may exist beyond celluloid.

And then, in college, I felt it fully, with H. A pure, romantic friendship. H was straight, and there was no sexual attraction between us, at all. But the love we had for one another was pure, kind and indefinable. We moved silently together along sidewalks and forest trails as much as we investigated our thoughts amidst that silence. Philosophy was the haze that floated around our heads. And we argued intensely, about the Cartesian Circle, or Kant's categorical imperative. But always, a physical affection. We spooned many nights during the friendship, mostly on a ratty couch in the living room of a cockroach-infested crash-pad we ignorantly called Guatemala and fell asleep with our noses burrowed in the others' hair. Another state of being. My *own* private Idaho.

One night, an argument we were having over ethics got heated—how culturally relative can a virtue be? We were sitting on opposite sides of the living room, leaning into the space of disagreement with the passion and youth that kept us both so lean. We could not stand down from our positions and ended with a frustrated stalemate, retreating and feigning sleep on our respective, separate couches across the room. And, it felt so wrong, to be so far away from a person I loved, especially while harboring something as jagged as anger. I stared up at the ceiling in the dark, marveling in the wrongness. And, in a perfect moment that boundaries can never cultivate, H whispered, tender, into the dark, "Come here." And, conspiring in the wave of that perfect, honest moment, I scooped myself over to his couch, nestled into his body, and fell asleep with his nose burrowed in my hair. Conflict not resolved, but more dis-solved. Love. Of all the memories of my youth, this one I file under "fearlessness" in my database.

There have been different kinds of whispers about Abraham Lincoln and his lifelong friend Joshua Speed. Accusations of them being secret lovers, because for years they shared a bed. Historians use evidence to argue that they were. Others use evidence to prove they were merely engaged in acceptable behavior of the time. My question: what does it matter? Do we understand more from this form of interrogation, or do we understand less? Is there anything to learn? May there even be danger in asking? Sometimes all that is needed to create a boundary is a fearful question.

And then, it became dangerous, with M. Pensive, spindle-haired, introspective M. Again, a journeyman with whom I walked alongside. Shared silence, a campfire lighting our faces and nothing else. M, who would waltz into the common room of his dorm, find me reading Neruda on the shit-brown sectional, and without pause collapse his head on my chest, and immediately find sleep. I would absently caress his hair with my fingertips while sounding the poet's words with my lips.

But maybe mouthing Neruda was too much, as my feelings for M moved towards a horizon that M never sought. And one night, with my desire and a trespassing body, that horizon became an edge. And, as with edges, a cut. I listened more to myself than I listened to our togetherness, and without a word spoken, we were done. And, as with edges, a fall. There is no farther fall than the one of shame.

I have to assign these men merely letters, out of respect for them, as it is possible that their minds have created a boundary that exists now, in their memory, that didn't exist, then: when boundaries weren't as much our concern. We often call this innocence. I don't want to give it a name, for as soon as we do, it is no longer there. It is changed, and becomes more the word than what it really was.

And now, this boundary. And thus, this fear. A river's edge, if approached too close, can sweep a body beyond itself, perhaps even into something as unknown as oblivion, but certainly into danger. So, there is this need for lines, for lines crossed, a need for safety. But once that fear draws those lines that never existed before, we become more aware of crossing them than we do the space in which they were drawn. Even the most consuming fire, if left unattended, goes out eventually.

As I've grown older, I have walked far from sight of the boundary's fine lines, a horizon disappeared, and now presume that any desire for intimacy must be entreaty of a trespassing body. It is safer this way. It is safe. I still remember the times in my youth when that was not the case. But now, I have cut that feeling out of me. I wonder if I could ever will it back. Can boundaries ever be erased once they are known? Can one ignore a river's edge once they've seen it?

Once Scott unearths ardor and Carmela in the Italian countryside, he ceases spooning with Mike. Once Abe married Mary Todd, he and Joshua shared a bed no longer. Was that the mapping of their river's edge, or was it more their move towards a different horizon, one I don't understand? I only know my own sight, and I tend to look more to the distance than to that which is close-up.

When I relocated to Los Angeles for grad school, one of the first things I did upon arrival was visit the Viper Room, the place where River Phoenix collapsed from the speedball that eventually took his life on Halloween morning, 1993. I stared at the dirty sidewalk in front of the unassuming club and mourned something more than the actor, his brilliance and even more than his influence on me. Without exactly knowing, I was mourning my own innocence, somehow, as if it were something that could suddenly collapse as well. And, in a way, it did. Innocence is viewing the world without so much as boundaries, to know something lies infinite beyond the horizon, to see life as a single continuous thing, including our relationships—the people we love, whether it be with our hearts or our hands or both. By the time I paid homage to Phoenix on the Sunset Strip, I had allowed my fear to build those boundaries with the definition of a river dividing two parts of the very same thing. I allowed fear to take my innocence and disappear along the quick-moving current.

Drinking with my grad school cohort, alone in a bar in Hollywood, I slurred on a cocktail napkin:

Boundaries are political. Love is not political. Lines drawn in love are blind.
Boundaries are political. Love is not political. Lines drawn in love are lies.
Boundaries are political. Love is not political. Lines are drawn in love all the time.

I gave it to one of my friends. In a different time, in an earlier time, I would have kicked his boot. I would have allowed myself to say, "I want to be close to you." He read the napkin silently, then slid it back over to me and said, "Nah. You may need this one day."

I think I understand what writing does. Lines, for the unlimited. This knowing has me forget to breathe. I lift my eyes to the current, follow it into the horizon, watch it never disappear through tears and ache again for firelight.

TRYING TO SHOVE OURSELVES BACK TOGETHER

(after *Hedwig and the Angry Inch*)

IN SUMMER 2018 a group of senators, led by California's Kamala Harris, introduced a bill that would require the U.S. census to solicit and record responses in our country's largest survey for a new category: gender identity. Forms for the census—which the Constitution requires every person in the U.S. to take part in—have long offered people the option to select "male" or "female" as their sex. Harris said, in a written statement, "The spirit of the census is that no one should go uncounted and no one should be invisible."

I'm curious what sort of spirit a census possesses. In general, it is the procedure of systematically acquiring and recording information about the members of a given population, usually one of a nation. It bears Latin derivation, with the earliest known Roman census administered by King Servius Tullius in the 6th century BC. Other known census efforts, however, began one thousand years prior, in Egypt. Intact records from the 1st century AD have been preserved in China. There are mentions of a census in Exodus. India performed a census around 300 BC during the reign of The Emperor Chandragupta Maurya.

The new bill does not clarify what response options for gender identity would appear on the Census Bureau's questionnaires. The agency would be asked to conduct research to come up with a plan to develop the new questions within a year after the bill becomes a law.

This bill arrives on the heels of what appears a movement to more accurately represent the complex of our culture, and particularly this aspect of human identity: gender. For so long, at least in the Euro-colonized U.S., male and female were the options available for both someone's sex—their biological attributes given them at birth—and their gender, an individual's performed characteristics of being.

My friend, Hollywood neighbor and fellow broke artist Cee had a personal visit during the 2010 census, "because I forgot to fill my form out." The representative was a skinny kid with pimples on his chin and a buzz-cut. Cee identifies as neither gender. So, when it came time for the sixth question on the census form, and only available to check were male and female boxes, Cee gawped at the representative with an open mouth. Buzz-cut was equally turkey-necked—it is rather difficult to assign Cee an apparent gender upon sight—so Buzzcut ultimately instructed, "Whatever it says on your birth certificate is what you have to check." Cee, not a stranger to public humiliations, explained to me over beers at our favorite dive, The Spotlight, "I wanted to cry, Miah. It's different when it's assholes heckling on the street, or homonormative dudes in West Hollywood. This was the government. My government. I love this country." And in the following elliptical silence, I knew Cee was discovering, in a deeper way than they had ever considered, that their country, in some ways, didn't love them.

This is changing, however, not just in America but around the world, if bureaucratic minutiae is any signifier, at least. Australians now can choose "X" as their gender in all government documents. In 2004, the Chiang Mai Technology School in Thailand allocated a separate restroom for kathoeys, with an intertwined male and female symbol on the door. In 2007 in Nepal, the supreme court ordered the government to issue citizenship cards that allowed "third gender" to be listed. In 2016, an Oregon circuit court ruled that resident Jamie Shupe could legally change gender to "non-binary." And, in 2017, my home state of California passed legislation implementing a third, non-binary gender marker on birth certificates and drivers' licenses.

Many socially progressive folks are clinking wine glasses with this recent development. The news excited me, as well. In the Bay Area, I have dozens of friends and colleagues who don't subscribe to "male" or "female." My friend

B was born with the biological attributes of a male but adopts the cultural characteristics of the feminine, including dressing, presenting as, and requesting to be referred to as "she/her." My friend T appears biologically and presents culturally female, but identifies as "they." My neighbor L desires no association to male or female and considers non-binary a suitable term. For these folks, it seems that the new census bill would be a step towards visibility, making them feel more considerable in the fabric of their culture, or at least more considered.

This occasion was not necessarily met with warmth elsewhere. When home for Thanksgiving, I caught up with my cousin Tammy. Growing up we were the closest in age, so I always felt a pull to keep tabs on her and made efforts despite her adoption of an evangelical form of Christianity that inspired in her a voracious judgment of others and the curious proclivity to bleach her hair two shades from translucent. Tammy was deriding one of her church friends named Terry, something about parking spots or baked goods, and in a requisite question as dedicated interlocutor, I referred to Terry as "they." Tammy snapped her head, her white bangs a crashing wave. "Oh, don't tell me you're one of *those* people." I countered that Terry was an ambiguous name and there had been no mention of pronoun, so I was simply ensuring I didn't mis-identify her friend. Tammy rolled her eyes with an exaggeration that had me wonder if it hurt. "Why do you liberals make everything so complicated? There is male and female. Okay, well, and some hermaphrodites." She brought her thumb and forefinger close to her left eye. "That's it. You people need to get over yourself." I wasn't sure if by saying "you people" she was referring to progressives, or queers, who, in her mind may all lump together, potentially with the folks who adopt a "they" pronoun, as well.

While I didn't challenge Tammy, knowing the confrontation would end with me self-righteous and condescending, and Tammy dislocating her eyeballs, I had my arsenal cocked and ready. Taking that Gender Studies course in grad school, running a queer literary press and simply living in the Bay Area, I was armed with what I thought was knowledge. In this circumstance, I could have presented all kinds of data, arguing for this third gender option as a mitigating effort against oppressive forces.

I would have begun with Aristophanes' speech from Plato's *Symposium*. In this dialogue, the playwright shares a myth on the nature of love: "The sexes were not two as they are now, but originally three in number; there was man, woman, and the union of the two, having a name corresponding to this double nature, which had once a real existence, but is now lost, and the word 'Androgynous' is only preserved as a term of reproach." Of course, I would have omitted that Aristophanes was a writer of parody. I then would have assured myself that myth was a tactical entry into the truth of things.

I definitely would have championed Judith Butler, as obligation to my six-figure college-loan debt. In their essay, "Performative Acts and Gender Constitution," Butler contends that "most actions are witnessed, reproduced, and internalized and thus take on a performative or theatric quality. Gender is a performative repetition of acts associated with the male or female. Currently, the actions appropriate for men and women have been transmitted to produce a social atmosphere that both maintains and legitimizes a seemingly natural gender binary. So, gender separates itself from solely being biological and sex related. Performance of gender creates gender itself." Our behaviors are prisms, ones that we walk into and refract beyond ourselves. Gender is not essential. It is socially constructed. Of course there may be more than two.

Nineteen century cultural critic K.H. Ulrichs argues the existence of a third gender, called Uranians. He adds there are residues of the other sex in each human, that there are the "germs" of both sexes within each embryo. Every human has these germs to various degrees. But they are deemed Uranians once they exhibit the desires of the residual in contrast to their apparent sexual body assignment.

Kanaka Maoli culture of Hawai'i have the Māhū, which means "in the middle." They served as priests and healers. Māhū were also valued as the keepers of cultural traditions, such as the passing down of genealogies. Traditionally parents would ask Māhū to name their children.

The Muxe of the Zapotece community in southern Mexico are assigned male attributes at birth but may assume characteristics associated with both males and females. They have traditionally been revered in the community, considered good luck.

The Hijra of the Indian subcontinent has a recorded history of four thousand years, most notably in the Kama Sutra, Mahabharata, and Ramayana. They are considered neither completely male nor female and live in specific communities led by a guru. They historically held important positions in court and administration—that is, until the British Conquest sought to criminalize them—and were sought out for fertility and birth-blessing rituals.

Indian photographer Dayanita Singh writes about her friendship with a Hijra, Mona Ahmed, and their societies' beliefs about gender: "When I once asked her if she would like to go to Singapore for a sex change operation, she told me, 'You really do not understand. I am the third sex, not a man trying to be a woman. It is your society's problem that you only recognize two sexes.'"

My own childhood. Before I even knew what sex was in any sort of embodied way, I felt discrete from both my boy and girl friends. When Amanda asked me to play grocery store, Juan would contest, "That's a girl's game," and when Juan asked me to play cops and robbers, Amanda would contest, "That's a boy's game." I wanted to play both, but more than that. I wanted to dance with ribbons in my hair, like Rainbow Bright, and I wanted to reconnoiter in the mud, like G.I. Joe; run around in my Aunt Donna's nightgowns because they made me feel pretty, but I also loved the coursing strength of my arms when a baseball bat made that cracking contact with the ball. Perhaps I am that third gender. Maybe I will check that box if and when it arrives on the 2030 census form.

But see, here's a problem. My Hollywood friend Cee would have been just as frustrated with the census visit by Buzzcut, even with the updated third option. Cee doesn't align with the term third gender. Or genderqueer, or non-binary, and especially "X." Cee's response: "It's all bullshit." So, what about Cee?

Maybe the answer is to provide more categories. I look to my data arsenal, and then some. The Dineh of the Southwest have four genders: male, female, male-bodied nadleeh, and female-bodied nadleeh. They were seen as distinct groups, each with their specific roles and duties in the society.

And the Buginese people of Sulawesi recognize five separate genders: makkunrai, oroané, calabai, calalai and bissu. One is considered bissu when all aspects of gender are combined to form a whole, and they take on the role of shamans. Calabai are biological men who take on feminine characteristics, and play an important role in wedding rituals. Calalai are biological women who take on masculine traits and perform jobs usually reserved for men. It was instructed that all five genders co-exist harmoniously.

19th century physician and sexologist Magnus Hirschfield called it "third sex" as an umbrella term for all types of "intersexes," but acknowledged a multiplicity. He became obsessed with creating a name for every type he studied, but soon became frustrated by the inability to categorize all permutations. He tried, though, and wound up with at least sixteen different possible types by the time of his death.

When I was eleven, my older brother led a family intervention in our small living room, nestled in the very heart of our trailer park. He asked me, "What are you?" He said that he was worried about me, and I believe this was true. Mama stood awkwardly to the side, picking her nails. I tried to answer— sometimes I wanted to be a girl, sometimes I wanted to be a boy. But in my limited vocabulary I failed to express that it never felt like that, exactly, like I at any moment preferred one side over the other. I also never felt like my biological attributes were unfitting. So, what was I? Not trans, not third gender, maybe genderqueer, maybe non-binary? In the small living room in Chesapeake Bay Mobile Court, in 1987, we knew none of these words, some didn't even yet exist. I wonder now which of his sixteen categories Hirschfield would have identified me.

Maybe we should have several words with adjacent boxes on our census forms, as many as will fit. Third gender, fourth gender, fifth gender, queer, transgender, genderqueer, gender variant, two spirit, genderfluid, neutrois, agender, androgyne, demigender, omnigender, intergender, pangender. Maybe the question should be its own form altogether.

Sadly, however, even the offer of several boxes to check still leaves us failing. There is a greater force that Cee, and we, and even the government officials, have to contend with. In Eula Biss' "Relations," one of her deeply vulnerable essays on race in America, she writes, "Our racial categories are so closely policed by the culture at large that it would be much more accurate to say that we are collectively identified." No matter how many categories we create, and determine ourselves to be, Biss continues, "Whenever we range outside the identity that has been collectively assigned to us, we are very quickly reminded where we belong."

Tammy, again. When faced with the "they" pronoun, or any consideration outside of the binary, she rolls her eyes and says, "Christ, what does it matter? Is it really such a big deal?"

The World Health Organization published a study in 2017 that determined that transgender, genderqueer and non-binary people are two to three times more likely to be victims of violent crime.

Gwen Araujo of Newark, California, was strangled, kicked and bludgeoned with a shovel by four men after they discovered Gwen had a penis. The defense argued that Araujo's deception shocked "ordinary human beings" beyond reason into murder. Sonia Rescalvo Zafra was killed in the Parc de la Ciutadella, in Barcelona, Spain, by six skinhead neonazis who kicked Sonia and a friend repeatedly in the head while they were lying on the floor. The conflict began when they asked if Sonia was male or female. William Lound was murdered during a planned attack by Lee Arnold, calling William "a little freak" as he stabbed William's head and neck, eventually scrawling "I always win" on the wall with an arrow pointing to the body. Alisha was shot seven times and died later in the Lady Reading Hospital in Peshawar, Pakistan. Hospital staff spent over an hour determining whether to place Alisha in a male or female patient ward. Bri Golec was stabbed to death by Bri's father who initially claimed it was "the cult" that had broken in and stabbed Bri. The cult he referred to was a local non-binary support group. Angie Zapata was beat to death with a fire extinguisher by Allen Andrade, who learned Angie was born with a penis. Shelby Tracy Tom was strangled by Jatin Patel after he noticed Shelby's sexual reassignment surgery scars. He claimed that Shelby caused him personal violation. He served four years in prison. Raina Aliev was hacked to death just after undergoing a sex change operation and getting married in Russia. Raina's family had called for the execution on national television. Kedarie Johnson was shot to death by Jorge Sanders-Galvez and Jaron Purham. The cases against the murderers were not prosecuted as hate crimes because Iowa state law only designates such with sexual orientation and not gender identity. Rae'Lynn Thomas was shot twice and then beaten to death by James Allen Byrd. Byrd called Rae'Lynn "a devil." Rae'Lynn's family requested the murder be investigated as a hate crime, but Ohio hate crime statutes do not cover gender identity. Islan Nettles was beaten to death in Harlem by James Dixon, who had initially been flirting with Islan. Lateisha Fobes King was shot by fellow classmate Brandon McInerney after asking Brandon to be their valentine. Dwayne Jones, 16 years old, was beaten, stabbed, and run over by a car in Jamaica after attending a party in a dress.

Notice I don't identify these people by gender or sex. They are dead, that is the only category that bears any relevance for this discussion. Their death is the real knowledge. And their names.

A student comes up to me after class. I have just assigned an excerpt from Judith Butler's *Gender Trouble*. Describing the reading, I had referred to Butler as genderqueer. My student asks, of the author, "If they are genderqueer, does that mean they're transsexual or does it mean they are bisexual?" I stood there, dumbfounded. Not by the ignorance of the student, but by my own. It was at that moment I realized, this rather innocuous moment, I had endangered Butler. No matter what, no matter how many names we give gender, no matter how many boxes we offer, the binary is there, embedded in the role of language. A checked box or an unchecked box. To check the box is to be. To not check the box is not to be. This, or that. One, or the other. After all the grad school classes and the chats with Cee, after the podcasts and articles and Ted Talks, it was my student's innocent question that had me realize how violent it all was.

I know that I am an entity in-between words, but very soon into my life I moved towards a—how I hate this word—"cis" presentation. I exhibit loads of feminine characteristics, but out of fear early on I emphasized the traits of a cis male. I always felt comfortable with my biological sex, and though I felt the variant constructions of gender flow through me, ungraspable as water, I wore clothes that signified male. I exaggerated my male identifiers, no doubt. I grew a beard. I did this to protect myself. From violence. Who knows what I would have become otherwise. That is not really important. What is more important, much more important, is that not all of us have the luxury—the privilege—that I did.

I chastise myself for ever using Butler as support for the third-gender box. I focused so heartily on the argument that gender was socially constructed—liberated from sex—I failed to recognize that, in the vein of social construction, gender isn't fixed in any way to be assigned a category, a checked box on a form, no matter the number of options. I once again—as I have so often in my life—mistook data for knowledge.

Plato understood the danger of forms. He speaks of them in his most urgent and well-known allegory. As familiar as I am with the cave, why do I keep staring at the wall of shadows?

What's more, social atmospheres change. A theatre critic will argue that a performance is never the same twice. Fads flood a high school cafeteria, hair styles rage in fall and become the stuff of ridicule in summer. Love promises eternity, and then ebbs. The prism might refract what moves through it, but what moves through it will change. The light will shift throughout the day. As permanent as a document can be, the paper will yellow no matter your efforts for conservation. Air and light are inevitable.

In *Cratylus*, another of Plato's dialogues, Socrates is asked whether names are "conventional" or "natural," that is, whether language is a system of arbitrary signs or whether words have an intrinsic relation to the things they signify. Socrates dismisses language, arguing that the thing itself is dynamic, while the name is not. He says, "Why give a thing a name that does not have a permanent nature?"

In March 2017, a coalition of Australian and Aotearoa/New Zealand intersex organizations released "The Darlington Statement," calling for an end to all legal classification of sex, stating that legal third classifications, much like binary ones, were based on structural violence. They argued that people should self-determine rather than be assigned. When I mention this to my class, a student says, "Maybe we need to go back to the beginning and ask ourselves why we classify at all." The class audibly agrees. After a brief pause, another student chimes in, "In this case its origin is based on love, right?" Some of the class nods, some stare into that invisible corner of youthful introspection, others chew their lips. No one speaks. And I don't have the certainty to, either. I dismiss class. I walk to my office and think of the names I've bestowed upon things.

Towards the end of his myth-telling in the *Symposium*, after Zeus has cut humans in half and pulled the wound closed to the belly-button, after he has threatened to do it again if we humans misbehaved, in which case we'd be "hopping around on one foot, looking through one eye," Aristophanes concludes, "Human nature was originally one and we were a whole, and the desire and pursuit of the whole is called love."

A MIRACLE OF MIRACLES
(after NOVA's *The Miracle of Life*)

THE FIRST TIME I SAW the actual birth of a child was in sixth grade sex ed at Harman Elementary, next to Chesapeake Mobile Court, where I was living with my mother and her new-ish husband, Bill. The class had already scarred my fragile ego by standing me next to Alfred Jump as demonstration of the varied stages of puberty in our young bodies, mine the example of a boy who hadn't displayed any of the characteristics of such a phenomenon. But that is a different essay, one perhaps more traumatic—and certainly more vitriolic—than this one.

The video we saw in sex ed was NOVA's 1982 classic *The Miracle of Life*, which chronicles the entire gestation of a single human organism from freshly ejaculated sperm to freshly birthed baby. I was so mesmerized by the complexity of the progressing stages, the catalog of chemical processes, by the *science*, that I even forgot for a moment how this class originated the new nickname I would suffer at the hands of mean girls and meatheads for the rest of the school year: little baldy.

The Miracle of Life was graphic for a pre-internet, pre-YouTube, 12-year-old without a household Cinemax subscription. This video *showed* stuff. The mother, a feather-haired woman who looked a lot like Princess Di circa fairy-tale wedding, was being encouraged to push by a smiley doctor who looked a lot like Sigourney Weaver circa *Aliens* Ripley. NOVA showed the crowning of the baby head-on, and the mother's private parts in all their bushy, ever-widening glory. The video ends with the baby's body eased out, followed by an immediate cut to being cradled alongside the mother, and this phrase: "The incredible journey of birth is complete." Other than the baby's head looking a bit gray in its first moments, the birth was…well…beautiful. The Ripley doctor was beaming in joy, the handsomely bearded father was mouthing "Wow," the soundtrack was swollen synth in a major key and the mother was laughing, face aglow, her lip gloss intact and her feathered hair wispily defying gravity. I think I even teared up at this final scene. I may have mouthed, "Wow," as well.

I remember my mother telling me about my birth. She said it was very fast, and when I came out I didn't cry. I simply came into the world, opened my eyes and was pleased. She said, "It was amazing. A miracle." The image I carried of this story was of me, radiant in my newness, looking Buddha-like, my legs folded in vajrasana. I was an easy labor, and I prided myself on this fact, that it in some way signified my overall personhood.

The next time I saw live birth was Stan Brakhage's 1959 experimental film *Window Water Baby Moving* in my Sophomore Art and Culture course. This was a very different experience than NOVA, with warm-toned lighting and quick jump cuts ranging from Brakhage's very pregnant wife submerged in a bathtub to middle shots of her belly to close-ups of her vagina during the big moment.

Now, I was 19 years old at this point. I'd heard enough to know that birth was a painful process, sometimes complicated, on rare occasions even dangerous. But I was male, an American male, and a homosexual male at that. I didn't have to think too much about pregnancy and birth. I never lounged on the grassy quad of my Georgia alma mater and pondered images of labor, whether inspired of my own doing or not. And the images I *did* possess in my database were of Princess Di and Sigourney Weaver over-smiling amidst 80s synthesizer-and-hair-spray oblivion, and my own celestial Buddha-birth. But now I had a new experience of birth with Brakhage's silent video: blood. Lots of blood, seeping out of his wife's vagina, before, during and after their daughter emerged, with various jelly-like and runny substances smothering the newborn's alien cone-head. And then the placenta squeezing out like an afterthought, a shockingly large, bloody, meaty mass that I imagined making a sound like caught catfish slapped onto the deck of a pontoon boat. I think I even exclaimed after class, "I can't believe all of that came out of her!"

There was more to this birth thing than I thought.

When a friend from high school had her first child a few years later, I went home for the Sip and See. Her friends were wearing pastel sundresses, fawning over the baby, cooing half-sentences: "So amazing. A Miracle," like a melismatic chorus. As a polite gesture, I asked what was most memorable about the labor, expecting an answer similar to my mother's, similar to all women I'd known who'd had a baby, where mother was exhausted but aglow, with a heartwarming simultaneity of cries and laughter. But not Tisha. With a signature deadpan look that she perfected alongside me during our rebellious teenage years, she said, "For real? I had to get twelve stitches. Dante was so fucking big he ripped the skin between my pussy and asshole."

And not long after that, my friend Sarah asked me to attend her childbirth. The father had ghosted her upon hearing the news that she was pregnant, and Sarah's Pentacostal South Carolina family pretended their 23-year-old college-educated daughter was not having a baby out of wedlock. Sarah was my good friend. Of *course* I would support her, hold her hand as I had seen done on every Emmy-nominated prime time TV show. And, now I knew more. I was ready for the blood, for the placenta. I wasn't going to be surprised or grossed out.

That baby was 9 pounds, 11 ounces. Sarah had a waist my arms could wrap around twice. When that baby started coming, so did everything else. First, Sarah peed. A lot. Pee was going everywhere. I thought it was going to hit the doctor's face it was so forceful. Poor Sarah was apologizing, but everyone kept telling her, *No, it's just water.* She even contested through gritted teeth, "I know I peed." But the doctors ignored her, told her to focus, to breathe.

But then little Taylor's shoulders got stuck, and the next thing I knew Sarah's feet were pulled to her ears, and everyone was telling her to push harder, push harder! The room was frantic, and Sarah was screaming so loud I thought her vocal chords were going to pop like guitar string. And then, the poop. Sarah was pooping, all over the place. Screaming and bleeding and snotting and pooping, folded up like a lawn chair. Wherever there was an orifice, something was coming out of it. Her body was completely out of her control. And it was disgusting.

Taylor was a healthy baby girl. Her face and body were wiped down. The delivery bed stripped and cleaned, Sarah rosy from the exertion, but calm. I was holding her hand. She was looking intently at me with remnant tears in the corner of her eyes, as if asking something of me—affirmation, confirmation? In the most sincere, beatific face I could conjure, I cooed, "So amazing. A miracle."

I was incensed. Why don't the great big *They* tell us this shit, this truth about birth? Why didn't NOVA at least show Princess Di with sweaty hair stuck in clumps to her forehead? Are they afraid we sixth graders won't want to have children if we see the real deal? And if this kind of revulsion is such a well-kept secret, what else are *They* not telling us about our futures? What other horrors are we waltzing into willingly, snowed by the glossy stories, the omitted details, the well-edited promotional videos?

Why do we curate the most immediate and animal of ourselves into something antiseptic? Why do we take a sort of cultural sandpaper to the representations of our biology, scratching smooth our bodies until they gleam with the gloss of *Cosmo* or *Vogue*? And what are we exactly buffing out? I ask this question to my LA friends over drinks at a local watering hole. Mel recoils at the question, as if envisioning all of the world's bodily functions erupting at once. Dana quickly replies, "Sin, Miah. Duh. You went to Catholic School." I stare at a water stain in the bar table. *Duh.* Of course. We make museum pieces of our bodies because art is a closer thing to God, and blood and snot and poop aren't, and we aim to be as close to our promised sacrality as we can, as often as we can, to summon that seemingly impossible worth.

All of these experiences shattered the image of my own birth, my exalted beginnings as a sitting lotus, another type of glossy magazine ad. Let's be real: I wasn't the only male who carried this inflated conceit about the splendid entry into their mother's world. She said I was a quick labor. Now, the thought of me shooting out of my mother's 5'2, 95-pound body like a Catapult pitching machine immediately filled me with terror. I knew now that the cervix had to dilate systematically in order for that large an object to pass through. I knew now that the pressure on the body is so great that most women will bleed, will tear, shit on themselves, piss on everything else. So, what happened when the baby also came quick? I was mortified that I may have torn my mother's asshole. That Thanksgiving I wanted the truth, however ugly.

I selected the day after the Thanksgiving meal, the flock of family gorging on Black Friday electronics sales at Walmart. Mama and I were not shoppers, and instead were playing a game of Scrabble that, of course, she was winning. I had been drinking wine, so it summoned in me a bit of courage. "Mama, you told me that I arrived really fast during birth. Wasn't that difficult?"

But all my mother said was, "You were a quick labor," her pale eyes determined to arrange seven tiles into yet another slaying of her English-major son.

I shook my head. "But wasn't it hard, you know, for your body?"

She smiled, "Miah, it was a miracle. A really amazing thing."

With the wine coursing through me, determination on my tongue, I pushed further, my mouth dilating with the taboo question. I wanted to punch a hole through the magazine ads of our biology, of our body-lives curated for the Second Coming. I needed to know just how traumatic giving birth to me was. I needed to know just how much pain I caused, how much embarrassment.

"Mama...did you poop?"

Her eyes reluctantly left the tile rack, she took a slow sip of her sweet tea, relaxed her shoulders into the high-back dining chair—as if she had expected this line of inquiry—sighed, and said, "You men ask the most irrelevant questions."

THE TREACHERY

(after Renée Cox's *Yo Mama's Last Supper*)

RENÉE COX'S *YO MAMA'S LAST SUPPER* is a full-color five panel photographic installation that features twelve men at a banquet table with the artist herself standing nude in the center, a white shawl draped over her outstretched arms, as if giving blessing. When the piece toured in New York City, it was met with fury by then-mayor Rudy Giuliani. He said that it was "outrageous," that it was "disgusting and anti-Catholic," that it was a gross misrepresentation of the original. Cox's initial reply to the mayor was, "Get over it. I don't produce work that necessarily looks good over someone's couch."

At a friend's BBQ in a sunny Oakland backyard, I struck up conversation with an acquaintance's 12-year-old daughter. She told me that she'd made the decision to play a nerd in high school and become a lawyer because she's "not pretty enough to do other things." I wanted to ask her, "Pretty enough for what?" but was so stunned by the frankness of her self-determined position in the societal pecking order that I let her continue on with the grocery list of imperatives for her guaranteed life success. Finally, after sharing the colleges she would attend (Berkeley and Columbia), where she would live (Manhattan), and what kind of law she would practice (environmental), I told her that I thought she was pretty. Her response: "Thanks, but my nose is too flat." I asked, "What do you think pretty is?" Without hesitating she said, "Taylor Swift."

I was walking along Merrimon Avenue in downtown Asheville with Pauline, my McGuffey's Family Restaurant co-worker and favorite smoke-break companion, when I waved across the street upon sight of my neighbor. Pauline gasped, "You know Jesus Guy?!" I laughed, "Mikey?" She looked at me with incredulity. "Come on. Long blondish hair, always in those sandals, kinda pretty? We call him Jesus Guy!" I shrugged. What I wanted to do was scoff, to summon my liberal arts rationale, to argue that Jesus certainly wasn't a shaggy-blond-haired, blue-eyed white guy. But decided against it because, shamefully, I realized I had often thought the same thing about Mikey, too.

When Aram and I broke up, lying in our bed in a tucked away bedroom of a tucked away part of Highland Park, Los Angeles, I was certain that it was not the end. I was certain. I knew what love looked like—human beings made songs, films, books, a catalog of culture on the matter—and our love fit the look: the serendipity, the wordless knowing, the close-cropped laughter. It was every third act in an atmospheric indy-film romance. So I waited for Aram to come to his senses. And waited. Stared at a ceiling fan for a week's worth of hours with the waiting. And a month later, thousands of revolutions and 25 pounds less, my certainty devolved into obsession, and my last words to him before he closed me out for good were lyrical incantations from highly recognizable and beloved love songs.

For his retelling of *The Passion of the Christ*, Mel Gibson dedicated himself and his 30 million-dollar budget to fastidious accuracy. He measured his film scenes in the approximate real-time of Jesus' last hours. He consulted with Biblical experts for exact textile replications in costume only filmed actors eating produce that would have been harvested during that era. He even had the script translated into Aramaic, Jesus' native tongue, a language long since diminished and spoken by only the smallest pocket of people in a far corner of the Middle East. And then, curiously, he cast Jim Caviezel as the title character. Irish and Slovak, blue-eyed Caviezel. Despite historical knowledge that it was uncustomary for men to wear their hair long in Judea at the time, Caviezel's Jesus sported luxurious shoulder-length tresses worthy of a Pantene Pro-V commercial.

René Magritte's *The Treachery of Images* hangs in the Los Angeles County Museum of Art. It is a painting of a pipe with the words "Ceci n'est pas une pipe" below, translated as "This is not a pipe." Concerning the painting, Magritte said, "The famous pipe. How people reproached me for it! And yet, could you stuff my pipe? No, it's just a representation, is it not? So, if I had written on my picture 'This is a pipe,' I'd have been lying!" Was this painting more warning than wax? Did Réne clutch the Old Testament—particularly the book of Exodus, particularly the Second Commandment—in his hand while holding his paintbrush in the other?

I look through all the pictures taken while Aram and I were together. We are laughing, all teeth and crow's feet. We are pressing our foreheads together, sharing a wordless knowing. We are akimbo in the thrill of our mutuality. There are no pictures of our disagreements, no record of the six-month slog into dissolution. Only a sequence of what was gleaming and sweet, along with the cooing comments of our three-thousand closest friends and acquaintances below. These are the documents of our history. For a while, a selection of them—the most convincing depictions of our love—were framed and hung over the couch.

When Giuliani accuses Cox's photographs to be a misrepresentation of the original, what is he referring to? The final dinner shared by Jesus' apostles? Wouldn't that have been a gathering of poor and shabby men eating a meager meal of bread and wine? We must all wonder what it really looked like. Unfortunately, there were no cameras in those days, no selfie sticks, no drones flying overhead. Our imagination is how we paint the moment. That is the beauty of our minds. But what happens when we don't use our imaginations at all?

When you see a lie over and over again, you begin to believe it is true.

What image comes to mind when you think of the last supper? More than likely, it is Da Vinci's legendary mural housed in the Convent of Santa Maria delle Grazie in Milan. DaVinci used Italian models and the current Renaissance fashions as source for his depiction more than he did history. He used the beauty of his mind. Doesn't the artist have the right to depict the subjects of their work in any way they choose?

I am writing this essay. I am representing Aram's relationship with me through the parallel device of Yo Mama's Last Supper. Is my rendering accurate to history? Not really. Is that possible? Not exactly. Does it matter? Perhaps.

We want to be the finger pointing to God, but we also want to make God herself, particularly a version that would glean the most likes. Which fails more? Da Vinci's *Last Supper*? Cox's *Yo Mama's Last Supper*? Gibson's film? Is this even the question to be asking? Perhaps that is what all art is: to figure out why we do it, in spite of itself.

What we can reason is that the last supper wasn't a bunch of long-haired Mikey-looking white men feasting at a lavish banquet table wearing crimson robes that swept the ground. What we can reason is that representation is always a lie. What we can recognize is the liberty of our imaginations. And yet, when Giuliani accuses Cox of her gross misrepresentation of the original, he in fact is referencing—as his original—a gross misrepresentation of the original.

Ceci n'est pas Jésus.

Taylor Swift currently appears on more magazine covers than any other celebrity. Her nose is thin, barely a sliver of flesh in such an eggshell face— breakable, hollowed, white.

Ceci n'est pas un beauté.

When you see a lie over and over again, you begin to believe it is true.

I listen to a lot of highly-recognized and beloved love songs. I watch a lot of packaged serendipity, close-cropped laughter, in my Netflix feed of independent coming-of-age gay romances. I see a lot of images made with cameras, drones, selfie-sticks, on two-dimensional screens. I see it again and again and again. Perhaps it is time for me to watch something else.

Perhaps it is time for us all to tell new lies.

LINE AND LOOP

(after Meredith Monk's *Turtle Dreams*)

IT BEGINS WITH GOING to the store.

Your mama has asked you to take the car and pick up some things at the local Giant supermarket. It is early summer in Maryland, and junior year already feels long gone. You grab the keys and step out into the still afternoon heat. As you move toward your mama's red pickup truck, a swell of cicadas wiggle their tymbals in the trees. It begins with one, but soon their 100-decibel abdomens quickly join in a concert of space that fills the whole world. You can't even hear the engine turn over their relentless sex buzz, and it hits you just how wild nature is, this cacophony, this overwhelming sound.

Just as you back out of the driveway, drops fall from the sky; one, then three, and within seconds the rainstorm dumps itself onto the earth. It is early spring in the North Carolina Appalachia. The tap and crackle of drop on metal meld into singularity. You turn on the windshield wipers of your rickety and very yellow Chevy Malibu and pull onto the mountain road. The rain is a constant, and the split rubber of the feeble wipers yields a rhythm of wheeze and thump, wheeze and thump.

Once parked outside of the grocery store, you run quickly to the entrance. It is a giant space. It is fall in Atlanta. The air is a shock of cold against your wet clothes from the rain torrent. You look around to figure what you need. Hundreds of people are clutching their baskets, pushing their carts, checking their lists made on notepaper, torn open envelopes, napkins. Children brandish sugary cereal boxes in front of parents. Babies are either laughing or crying, which has always been hard for you to differentiate. It seems all too much, and you feel the urge to turn back. But you find cadence in the squeal of errant wheels, the thin clang of carts bumping, the lifeless steps of zombie-shoppers, and you merge into the throng and find your bounty.

The checkout line is your least favorite place in the store. The neutered portrait of people waiting always incurs in you a misery. The beeps of barcodes on products scanned and swept across the conveyor, the clip-clapping of long, manicured nails on register keys, and those same beeps of the barcodes and nails

on keys at the other checkout aisles forms
layers upon layers of beeps and clicks. The
tenor and tempo dishearten, this monotony,
this unnatural sound, this lack of something
that you might call soul. You remember your
brother always pocketing gum in the aisle
and slipping out without notice.

You drop into your taupe Elantra with bags
of fruit and ramen and Kettle-Style potato
chips and crank the ignition. The Drake song
on the radio immediately has you grooving,
wiggling in your seat as you cruise down
Sunset Boulevard towards your small
Hollywood cottage. There is the driving
metronome of a beat, and then overlaid
sounds to other rhythmic counts, grumbles
and snaps. Something ordered and something
wild. You summon a memory. Not really a
memory but an impression, a patterned sound
similar to the layered sequence of clicks and
beeps from a grocery store checkout line.

The Ancient Greek poets believed that
humankind struggled between its two natures:
that of the Dionysian and the Apollonian.
The Apollonian was our reason, our civic life,
our grids and lines. The Dionysian was our
fury, our lust in the forest, our bumblebee
flight. Line and loop. Metronome and
Melisma.

You have often confused the Santa Ana winds whipping through the iconic Hollywood palm trees with a rain-stick played in an Athens, Georgia Widespread Panic concert.

You saw a dance performance in San Francisco set only to various recorded birdsong, and you had never before cried so much in public.

You were once caught by your co-workers absently dancing to the rhythm of printing syllabi on the department office copy machine. The evidence is on YouTube.

At home in your San Francisco flat, the groceries you bought earlier are now laid out in matching bowls and platters. You have friends over for game night; this time, at the pleading of one of your actor friends, Cards Against Humanity. At one moment during the game the phrase card is, "Instead of wine for communion, priests now serve to children_____?" When you throw the "an unexpected finger in the anus" card down on the table, the laughter first begins with one recovering Catholic friend, but soon everyone is laughing with abandon. It apexes and then diminuendos gradually, with mere soft chuckles following up the rear of the swell. You recall at that moment, in vivid memory, the wave of cicada buzz in the summer sky of your youth.

The end of a spring Georgia day in a friend's Oconee lake house, you are in bed, allowing your body to maneuver its slowdown. You drift in and out of untethered thoughts: impressions of your middle-aged marriage, books to write, people to email. Suddenly the glimmer of a rhythm has your head rolling side to side in your bed. An image of Chiquita, your old, very yellow Chevy Malibu emerges, the windshield, the broken wipers on full power in the rain. You hold the memory, the movement, a squeaking upside-down, lopsided pendulum, and the longer you hold, the more an existent sound floats into the foreground: creek frogs chirping just beyond the lake house property line.

Eventually, you fall asleep in this world of rhythms; these rhythms, the world. Apollo could see the reason of the universe in the tessellation of a leaf, and Dionysus plucked the leaves from the grape arbor and garlanded his diadem. Line and loop, metronome and melisma, humanity and nature. What are their differences as you sleep? What are their differences at all?

THE BEING OF SUCH
AN UNLIKELY THING

THE LEG LAMP—its fishnet stocking, flapper fringe and high heel—is almost an exact facsimile of Old Man Parker's "major award" in *A Christmas Story*. I am marveling almost as much as Old Man himself, delighted by the being of such an unlikely thing. My tuxedo shirt's untucked, my hair tousled, I am beaming with a readiness for something new. Mama is looking lovely in cream, and the gift is a dream.

This photo finds itself in different rooms, depending on where Mama moves next. For now, it rests on a desk in her living room. My high school graduation from Cardinal Gibbons. We have returned from the ceremony, and the lamp is my present. Mama wanted to get me something I'd take to college, knowing I wasn't much for stuff unless it made me laugh or made itself useful. What better than this? It remains to this day my favorite gift. I set it on a table in the center of my dorm room window once it made its way down to Atlanta.

The afternoon is warm and swollen with the promise of rain, and the bugs are chirping fast to get some sex in before the storm. The trees beyond my grandfather's yard begin to blink. He is still alive, my father's father, though my grandmother has been dead for a handful of years, and Aunt Donna and Uncle Ray moved from the back house to the front. I lived here once before, after I left Hawai'i with my father and before I moved to be back with my mother. I know this place well—the woods, the barn, the concrete porch that connected the two houses that smelled like dog urine. I learned how to swim in my aunt's above-ground pool.

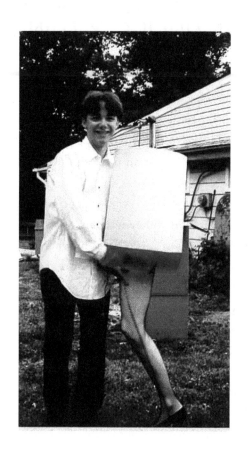

I learned how to drive a tractor. Ten years later, my mother has moved into the back house, and I am here again at the end of my childhood.

Mama and I moved around Maryland often for those handful of years. From the trailer park to Pasadena, to Granny's Glen Burnie breezeway, to the Baltimore projects, to the Ferndale cottage, and now here. Six homes in seven years. Each time she would say some variation of, "I'm tired of this fucking place." I was complicit in her declaration. We both were wanderers by nature, but our mobility wasn't out of want.

Before graduation, before I began high school, before I moved back with her, my mother met Bill Hibbs. He was a Marine, like my father. They met and married in that wrinkle of time when my mother wasn't around. Bill was handsome and charismatic and, most of all, strong. Strong enough to balance my body with one arm. Strong enough to, from a single punch, break the jaw of a man who fender-bended him in a parking lot. Strong enough to lift my mother clear off her feet by the neck, when his tinny suspicions echoed off the tops of empty beer bottles. He suspected she was cheating on him, but the malefactor was the paranoia characteristic of latent schizophrenia.

Five years before my graduation day, on March 30, in the finale to a series of escalating violence, Bill came home reeking of booze, shoved my mother into her car, and drove towards the place he planned to kill her. He detailed to her how he was going to do it while she lay stuffed in the passenger floorboard. It is only by luck and the hawk-like spotting of an off-duty, plain-clothes cop that my mother did not end up dead in a ditch.

Because they were married, Bill was not sent to jail. Because of our patriarchal judicial system, Bill was not sent to jail. And while my mother sought refuge, obtained a restraining order, Bill freely followed—with his body, his voice, his iniquity. He spent nights parked outside my Granny's house, far away enough not to trespass, close enough to terrorize. Calls in the middle of the night to prove he knew where we'd moved. I could no longer ride the bus. One afternoon my 7th grade teacher, Mrs.

Johnson, asked me why I did so poorly on her science test—"You seem distracted lately"—and I cried alone against the smudgy glass of the middle school lobby doors, waiting for my police escort to take me "home." The phone calls, the unexpected cameos, the threats had my mother's nails bitten to the quick, and so we moved, and we moved—in some ways to evade him, in some ways, I believe, to evade her shame. I don't know why, but I felt my mother blamed herself for what happened. I only realized later that's what most battered women do.

Shortly after we moved to our Ferndale cottage, my mother happened upon an empath named Margaret. A small, knitted-sweater woman who could have been someone's grandmother, someone's macaroni casserole recipe, someone's Avon calling. Sweet, intent, lively eyes. When I ask my mother how she and Margaret met, she can't recall. At a grocery store checkout line? A street corner? An ad in the back of *The Baltimore Sun*? Mama has no clue. She was looking for something, and it obviously wasn't lost. She became part of Margaret's meditation gathering, several women assembled monthly from across the county. Margaret soon implored my mother to have me join—imagine it, a congress of middle-aged women and me, a late-blooming high-schooler. We sat in a circle, and "went down" into our minds to mine images. When we surfaced back, we'd brush off what we dug up from the deep end. In one of these sessions, called Love Throne, we focused energy on whomever sat at the head of the table, and shared what roused. Margaret told us to use hope as our eyes while our eyes remained closed. There was such a hope in all of these women, and my hope was to open my mother back to the world. After that horrible March 30th day—the Ides of March we called it—she closed up like a fist. I hated Bill most for this, and hated myself for feeling so helpless. During a Love Throne for my mother, the women conjured the color purple, a house on a lake, a porpoise, trees on a riverbank. I summoned an oyster shell. Margaret said I had a gift for reading. Margaret told me that one day my mother would lay the memory of Bill on a leaf and let it float along a river and never wonder where it ever went.

There is a hope in moving. It has us focus solely on what's next. Each place, a matter of something new. Each place, leaving something behind. Maybe even forgetting.

On a spring evening of my freshman year in Atlanta, my dorm room phone rings. I hear "Gerbil?" on the other end, a nickname Bill Hibbs gave me years before, when he had the right to give me one at all. That voice, at once familiar and foreign, now rose in me a storm that I presumed I'd long since withstood. I slam the receiver down with such a rage, such a want to send the hate along the phone line and take violent shape at the other end, that the table teeters. And my leg lamp, my beloved graduation gift, perched confidently on that table, falls and fractures in five places. I later choose to view this moment as liminal, a ritual, something dug up from the deep end, the being of such an unlikely thing.

My mother is moving again, this time to an Alabama river. "I'm tired of this fucking place," she says, and by place she means thirty years of Baltimore winters, Baltimore grit, Baltimore bullshit. But she also means the memories. She knows her life there is a patchwork of fractures, with each mending weaker than the last. I don't know, perhaps this is true for all of us. Maybe she will move to Alabama, and the warmth will loosen her fist. Maybe one day soon, a day not unique to others she will enjoy away from most of her life, she will walk to the riverbank, and she will launch a leaf, a thousand leaves. Maybe each leaf will carry with it something that needs to go. Maybe one of them will be the shame she's shouldered all these years. I am moved to tears simply by writing the hope of this. That she will drop that leaf in the water and turn back without watching it disappear down the current.

SEE YOU WHEN I SEE YOU

(after Peter Weir's *Gallipoli*, or maybe it's really
Albinoni's "Adagio in G Minor")

I AM WALKING around my new neighborhood in Asheville with my friend and roommate M the morning after a soft-fallen mountain snow. Together, we had moved up from Atlanta, I to run from a man or myself, I wasn't yet sure, she to find certainty somewhere, only certain it should be with me. As people do when walking through a fresh blanket of snow, we were reminiscing. Cue the cello.

M grew up in one single house in one single suburb in Georgia, so my childhood, with its frequent chutes and ladders, was a luge of curiosity. This time, of Hawai'i. Of the military base. Of the last time my family was all together. I recounted all I could. The shore where Mama and I would walk and stand ankle deep in the ends of waves, staring out to the barely-there splice of two-tone blue, an earth-sized Agnes Martin. The squat K-Bay store from which my brother stole peanut butter cups. The PX. The arcade. The duplex on Canney Circle. The living room, the dining room, the gecko that ran across the back wall at approximately noon every day. The hallway. The bathroom on the left that Mama tropicalized—painted parrots on the walls, a green shower curtain with palm trees. My parents' bedroom, and my brother's on the right, and mine. And. And, where was Shenandoah's, my older sister's?

I stop walking. M stops too, with expectant eyes. We are several blocks from our new house, the sidewalk buried in a thin white pack lightly crunching under our feet. I am facing a stand of trees, cold, and frozen with the failing of my memory. Where was Shenandoah's room?

I call my brother and ask him the question. We do not talk often in these days, the frequency of his own running over the years—from creditors, from scorned women, from the law—leaving a list of phone numbers long void. This time, he sighs heavy, and says, as he often does, "Miah, she doesn't exist." In previous instances, when I had tried to talk to Chris about Shenandoah, I'd grow teary and hot with this stubborn disregard for our sister, but now I heard something ring like truth in his words, his tired sigh a crack of light through a door in a room long dark.

Back at the house, I catalog my memories of Shenandoah. Of her under my sheets reading *Oliver Twist* with a flashlight, her auburn hair a cascade along the pages, tickling my forearm. Of us dancing on the bed to my Cyndi Lauper and Prince records. Of playing Grocery Store, where I'd tally the price of plastic food on the Texas Instrument adding machine at the desk in my room.

The night she ran away. My father announced he was reassigned to a base in Virginia, and he was to send me to live with my grandparents in Maryland. I returned to my room. Shenandoah became angry tears, said she refused to go, the island was her home. I said I would run away with her, but she shook her head, climbed through my window and slipped away, her hair trailing behind like the train of a wedding gown. No, not that. This: the retreating lip of a wave's end upon sand.

"See you when I see you."

"Not if I see you first."

In all of my memories of Shenandoah, it is always only us, always in my room. She doesn't help me make pancakes in the kitchen, doesn't walk me to school. I squint hard to recall a memory where we are with my parents, on the beach with Mama, in the back yard with Chris, but there isn't one. We are always alone. I get a blistering headache realizing this. Perhaps the world outside was too hostile, or the cinema of her could only be screened on the walls of my bedroom.

And, somehow, sometime after she slipped out my window in Kane'ohe and before I reunited with my mother three years later, Shenandoah died. I don't recall how I knew this, how it became known to me. There is no recollection of the exact moment. There is no funeral, no specific time of mourning. There is only the knowing. And in that knowing, I understood I could never talk about Shenandoah with my mother. The pain of her name would be too great. I even wrote a poem about her muted death in college, and it was published in the campus literary magazine. I think it won a writing prize. Art is a lie that tells the truth.

Shadows and light, electrical impulse, chemical, an open file. A perception. A projected image, subservient to language. But what was the name of this file? And from where in my database did I conjure this?

At least a poem, in itself, recognizes that it is the shadow of the cave and knows it relies on the firelight. But what of a myth born from nothing? What is the light source casting that shadow?

It took another few years after my walk around snow-blanketed Asheville to fully acknowledge that Shenandoah was only real in the way a story on the page—or art—can be real. The grief of my own deception was too much and spread too wide, and I avoided it. I hadn't understood the beauty of my mind, then, only its treason. That would take much more time. Indeed, it's still a realization in progress.

When you run, you think of your memories as behind you. You can't know if they are running after, but you trust they fall behind. I had to escape her, the myth of her, the way she had slipped into my room, as easily as she slipped out through my window.

So I ran. I guess I ran to Asheville. I certainly ran to Los Angeles. I lived in seven locales in five years. I ran, even when I realized what faced me was not a memory at all. It was shadow. How fast could I run? As fast as a leopard. How fast would I run? As fast as a leopard. And I did. And the only thought amongst the breathlessness: what else in my database was not real? What files could I trust?

I was a child when Shenandoah died the first time. And I was 28 when she died for the last. That required a couch on a friend's porch and a stillness I had never known before. But that story belongs to another essay.

The first person I shared this death with was my friend M. After all, it was the walk in Asheville with her years before that cracked open my mind, that had me look down at my running feet. M could only see the lie in it all and felt betrayed. It is sometimes easier to feel a single thing that drives you in one direction than be pulled nowhere with many, and M drove as far as she could away. I didn't try to follow, because I understood, and was too weighed down by shame to ever catch up.

Only years later, newly thirty, still ashamed of—not yet amazed by—my capability to fully fabricate a life so real, did I mention Shenandoah to my mother. We were playing a game of Yahtzee at the kitchen table during a visit for the holidays.

I tried not to betray my anticipation. "Mama, does the name Shenandoah mean anything to you?"

Without looking away from her scorecard, the five di penned in her cupped palms as if holding a small wild bird, she said, "Sure. It was going to be your name if you were born a girl."

THE PERFECT MOMENT

(after Robert Mapplethorpe's *Self-Portrait with Whip*)

I CURRENTLY LIVE in the Divisadero/Lower Haight district of San Francisco, a spillover neighborhood nestled between tie-dyed Disneyland-ed Haight-Ashbury, the Castro gayborhood and the historically black cultural center of the Fillmore. The location makes for a motley glory of characters sharing sidewalks: Brigitta, the Rasta organic-lotion-maker; Devon, the fire-eating middle-school math teacher; Bob, our whip-smart snarky landlord who helped elect Harvey Milk; let alone my own household of a Mexican-Guatemalan husband, Malaysian asylee artist and tatted-and-pierced activist Berkeley doctoral candidate. Everyone is hyphenated here.

When I first moved to the neighborhood a decade ago, I found it to be the perfect moment—moving to the city I loved with my gut and to a pocket of it that contained a community art space, Ethiopian restaurant, discount produce market, dive bar with two-dollar drafts and lifer bartenders and Sam's corner store that defied its size with an abundance of needs all on the same strip.

But the neighborhood is changing, much like the whole city. The tech economy is booming, and those who are riding this millennial Wall Street wave bring a very different sheen to the water. It has become wealthier, more white-collar, more white-washed, more white. And with that, an exodus of people that attracted me to the city in the first place. It is true what all the magazine articles and culture blogs say: San Francisco is losing something. But what, exactly?

Vincent, a bondage enthusiast who runs a Burner collective down the street, hangs explicit close-ups of nude models sucking dick, finger-fucking and fisting on the walls for the Divisadero Art Walk. I am handing him nails as he grumbles between hitting the hammer, "This neighborhood is getting so polo shirt. We need some Mapplethorpe shit to smack these bitches awake, remind them what this town is about." The weight of my nod is deliberate, one of insider knowledge—the image, the issue, all of it. "Now more than ever," I say.

Mapplethorpe's self-portrait is stark, high contrast, painting his shadows into void spaces: armpit, anus, brow. His back is crouched and bent, a strange shape of the body. His ass is exposed and squared and center; a tail slinks from inside, along the foreground, and out of sight. Gaunt face with features pulled forward to a point. This body shape, and this tail: one may think a rat, some kind of animal. But the tail is a black leather whip, and his chaps and vest are black leather, another animal. His right hand clutches the whip just before it disappears inside of him, and he looks directly into the camera, feral, almost sinister. Yet another kind of animal.

The first time I saw this photograph was in college. I was reading about the X Portfolio in my Photo History class. I winced, and an electric pinch ran through my limbs. It was the phantom pain of my naïve queer sympathy, pity for a man who lost his way, or something more baleful. I watched the fearful news, memorized the 90s AIDS PSAs. I knew what became of this man and somehow colluded his death with this image. That he would make this image at all was a kind of death.

I was very young.

In the years of Crisco and Disco, Mapplethorpe was introduced by then-lover Jack Fritscher to the Mineshaft, the members-only Meatpacking BDSM sex club that inspired dungeon love and piss-play, the Village People and jail-cell fetish, Foucault and Freddy Mercury. With his Hasselblad and handsome face he invited this night-life with flashbulb light. And part of that night, that life, became his own, like a picture in one's pocket.

In 1998, a decade after Mapplethorpe's death, Warner and Berlant wrote the essay "Sex in Public." It wasn't really about sex in public, but that got our attention. Indeed, that was the reality of the essay. Sexuality is mostly a public act—chivalric gestures, kneeling for the popped question, white lace and taffeta, bachelor parties, the white picket fence and certainly knowing that when you fuck missionary and cum inside it is to make a baby, and that growing belly is proof. All public. All white. But the world of Mineshaft Manhattan in the time of Mapplethorpe was private: in the shadows, leather and black.

At the same time Mapplethorpe sought a refuge in New York basements and blinds-drawn windows, in an effort to challenge San Francisco City Hall's defamation of a similar community on the other side of the continent, organizers created what is now the Folsom Street Fair, which brought the leather daddies, the piss pigs, the subs, doms and in-betweens, the Vincents, into the soft embrace of NorCal light. People gawked at the audacity, clutched their proverbial pearls, as ass-less chaps and nipple tassels paraded down one of the city's major arteries and the blood quickened with cock-ring vendors and panels on lube utility. Yet, people came—they certainly did.

Before sight of the photograph, before knowledge of the Fair, my world was Baltimore Catholic, and the body was dubbed a temple. Meaning, the body was sacred. Meaning, the body was only entered for the love ritual. Meaning, sex was our animal selves. A private animal. And even though my classmates and I rolled our eyes at the archaic sentiment, even though we all silently acknowledged that we masturbated every day, that we experimented with the girls of Seton Keough down the street (or fantasized about the boys experimenting with the girls of Seton Keough), we blushed as well, felt the twinge in our gut. Our body gave our shame away in some fashion.

From Berlant and Warner: "Making a queer world has required the development of kinds of intimacy that bear no necessary relation to domestic space, to kinship, to the couple form, to property, or to the nation." Straight folks have diamond rings and priests, a single red rose and The Supremes. We queers sought to conceive our own expression since none of those things were designed for us. That is largely what San Francisco was for a perfect moment, a bunch of loose change that didn't fit into a designated slot, and so they rolled west to create their own economy, their own public, South of the Slot.

My friend Kevin. We were waiters at a hip Atlanta bistro close to my college. Tall, football shoulders, forearms like polished ebony bedposts. He slung sandwiches and his imaginary wig, swishing across a floor like the song played only for him—a liquid body that poured sweet into open hands. I loved him dearly, but sometimes as he flooded a sidewalk or spilled himself into a store, I would feel my eyes roll for onlooking queers, a performance of *I am not like him*. Yet, if a frat boy or high-hair heckled, my same eyes would burn a hole into their polo shirt to arrest their ridicule. This duplicity didn't escape me, both this protective defense and wish that Kevin would tone it down sometimes.

I felt the same way the first time I attended Folsom. I was 22 years old, a twink, a cub, a stringing of lingo from a most colorful lexicon. The porn stands, the sex toy demonstrations, the sex, was dizzying. I was at once pulsing with the power I found in the street, but the Catholic school boy gurgled up, and I cowered as I walked through the crowd. I saw deviance. I saw darkness. These people had somehow lost their way. And after a man sporting a leather harness with his dick in his hand tapped me on the shoulder and asked if I wanted a taste, I breathlessly bee-lined for my hostel bed.

I was very young.

But see, Mapplethorpe wasn't just fucking; he was fighting. In New York, Ed Koch was a spineless Hercules charged with cleaning the stables to rid itself of its animals, and Robert didn't want to be swept away by a river. Imagine a river sweeping away all the rats of Manhattan, those trapped in a mineshaft. And San Francisco was fighting, as well, by ascending to the streets before the flooding trapped them all. It was the way to survive. I only learned this much later. I wish I had learned it sooner.

Kevin eventually retreated back home. He missed the family that saw his swish as a fuck you to a God that he very much believed in. And so, still lonely in Atlanta, policed even by those in his own community who, desperate, built plastic white fences around their basement flats, he packed away his wig, straightened his shoulders and squared back to South Carolina. And a light went out of him faster than a flood could sweep a street.

Times Square cleaned up not with water but with a flood of unnatural light, the dark of the night completely stripped away. It now exhibits a soulless glow, a spotless silver and glass, with tiny glimmers of a history blown out with neon advertisements, heteronormativity in LED. Now, it is a city in constant exposure, a constant public, and one that glares. San Francisco suffers the same—the sheen of the Salesforce Tower, the gleaming metal and glass of an unchecked industry, shiny as polished coin.

I was blind that first time at the Fair. The monochrome lens of my Catholic upbringing had me only see the black of the leather, the shrouded sex, the darkness that doctrines edify so well. What I didn't see that day was the color, the range of love that now had a place to be in a natural light. A different kind of public. Natural. Indeed, I now know this is one perfect moment that suffers no loss. In fact, it is all about finding, finding one another, and having the choice whether to remain in shadow or to walk in the light. A choice. I only wish that Kevin had seen Folsom before he succumbed to the ridiculous shame felt by so many queers for just being who they are. If only he could have flipped his wig once on that street, to embody, fully, the temple that was his self, a sacred thing. That beautiful animal.

Mapplethorpe looks right at me. You think the center of the photograph is his ass, but no. Look closer. It is the hand that grips the whip, like a talon, the whole arm active, a full control. And now, the look is not sinister at all. It is a challenge, daring you to tell him to tone it down. Daring you to dismiss his presence. That he is here, just as much as the frat boy, the high-hair heckler, and you and I.

We need to hang these fierce looks on the walls of our beloved towns before they suffer from too much polo shirt. Now more than ever.

Divisadero has become, in the words of realtor websites, "hot." The community art space is now a fashion boutique, the produce market a five-dollar pour-over coffeehouse. Brigitta moved her shop to Oakland. And

Vincent recently packed up and complained all the way to Portland. Change is inevitable. I get it. Cities change, certainly. But it isn't the change that makes my head so heavy. It is what we are losing in the midst of this: the loose change, the motley glory, that collective push against the conformity that threatened so many of our lives. Most tech bros don't know this because they've only known a picket-fence public and are safely oblivious within the privilege. They can't acknowledge San Francisco as a sanctuary, because they can't even see the threat we're protecting ourselves from.

Fuck white lace.

Mapplethorpe died at exactly the age I write this essay. This fact doesn't escape me. What have I done to counter the pressures of the picket fence, for not only people like Robert and I, but all those who don't want to kneel? What, write this essay? Perhaps. What I do know is that when I catch myself rolling my eyes, when I judge those who love differently, when I blush at the sight of my own body—all things I still catch myself doing—these are the moments I now feel shame because I understand it is weakness. Now when I walk into the swollen throng of Folsom, I recognize it as human resilience. Love is resilient. And Folsom may be a lot of things and certainly has changed over the years—just like San Francisco. But it continues (and must continue) as a fuck you to the forces that made me, made Kevin, made Robert afraid of their own hearts, by making public all the ways that love exists. It is, indeed—leather and lycra, harness and heartbeat—what love looks like.

LEAVING A MARK

(after Felix Gonzalez-Torres' *Untitled, 1991*)

THERE IS A BILLBOARD. A white bed, rumpled white sheets and white pillows, in a white room. The pillows have deep hollows, impressions, where a heavy head would lay in its comfort. But the bed is empty. White.

"Is that an ad for fancy sheets?" asks a fellow student. We are in a shabby corner of 90s Brooklyn, on a high-school field trip, going somewhere, I forget. This is all I remember about any of this trip, except for the spring New York air, the urine and the black tar tang of the river brack, of a climb into the crown of Liberty herself.

I can't stop staring at the image. I feel its loss. I somehow know the people who aren't there, without ever seeing them. It is a false knowing. I am 16.

Felix Gonzalez-Torres created this billboard to honor his lover, Ross Laycock, who died of AIDS-related complications. He said of his work, "Above all else, it is about leaving a mark that I existed: I was here. I was hungry. I was defeated. I was happy. I was sad. I was in love. I was afraid. I was hopeful. I had an idea." Felix died four years later, from "AIDS-related complications."

In the gay community we have our first stories, like any other: first kiss, first love, our "first time," but we have others ones, too: our coming out, our second "first time," our first hate crime, and our first death from AIDS. Mine was Michael, who lived across the hall in my college dorm, who came over at three in the morning to ask if he could cuddle, just cuddle, nothing more. Who had smelly hobbit feet. Who went to class donning an apron that said, "Kiss Me. I'm Irish." Who wrote me unrequited love poems and left them on my empty pillow. Scrubby fuzz on his chin, gap-teethed, grinning when he drank gin in a plastic flask, urging to us all the virtues of pure democracy. Five years later he was found dead in his hotel room in Washington, D.C. Working as an aide for a Georgia state senator's campaign. His body lay in the middle of the king, legs together, arms at his side, little plastic baggies, a spoon, a rolled up twenty. He had been diagnosed three weeks before. It was the 90s. We thought AIDS was a death sentence, and Michael decided to finish the line himself.

My generation was that in-between: after the education and before the hesitant sigh of relief, before Atripla and Videx and Emtriva and Zerit and Ziagen and Retrovir, before PrEP and Truvada and ARV. We had condoms and celebrities, PSAs and polished hair. And the word death. Death. In pink helvetica. In essence, we were terrified to have sex. But we were alive. We were safe. We did everything safe. I prided myself on doing everything safe.

My roommate, Irwan, is also of my generation. He went to art school—a painter. Then he stopped. Now he cooks. Rice, spicy noodles, curries that tear away the tops of the tongue and meat. Lots of meat. Busies his hands. Hums to himself to block out other noises.

He didn't want to know. Whatever the virus was cooking in his guts, he pretended wasn't there, the hiss inside, in his ears. He sang louder, in clubs with their bass thicker than the blood he never tested, in squealing bars, in cloudy porn shoot bedrooms. Then, another image, an abacus of him dying, six T-cells, 98 pounds, two weeks to live, a countdown, beads sliding along string, a litany of Latin syllables mapped over his body, his throat, his skin, his stomach waging war with the hiss that folded out of sound and into a breath heavier than any sex he ever had. In the generation before us, Irwan was supposed to die. But he didn't.

Torres created many works about the absence of his lover. One was a giant pile of Hershey Kisses in the corner of the gallery, the glinting silver chocolate bulbs, Ross' favorite, each glint a cue in the dint. The viewer was instructed to take. Eat. Then toss the wrapper in another pile, a smaller one. Little silver scraps. Rubbed to tiny balls by the pointed fingers of those very much alive.

> Dear Felix,
> Now, in the ground, then, on the bed, which were you walked on the more?

Irwan quit making art after his diagnosis. That is, save one work. A small painting, on wood, the top of a pill box, in a hospital pink background, with the first letters of each day, one on each flap: M, T, W, T, F, S, S. The hiss. I wondered with indignation why he quit making art. I feel the answer lies in this last painting, somewhere in the names of days. I stare at the little boxes with their letters, planned, filled with pills, his life. His only way to life. A different kind of death.

Michael's head pressed the hotel bed's pillow, did it not? With no lover next to him. Imagine the photograph. A bed. A pillow. A billboard never made. Is it easier to know the impression of two? Is it more painful to see the hollow of one? One without the other makes the one alone, unknown. Is that the hiss?

The pillbox. It tells me. Art has changed. The reminder is not the loss, but that we now are alive. What of this difference? Pillow to pillbox, death to some kind of life. Can art leave a mark on behalf of lives not gone, but unseen? Is that where the suffering lives on? An AIDS-related complication.

I did everything safe. I am healthy. I have pride. I have been in the crown of Liberty herself. And the view from there is lonely. I crawl onto my bed and impress my whole body, pitch my head, dig in deep. My false knowing. I have pointed the finger many times. And the finger that points forgets that the only thing true is the finger itself.

MAKE SURE TO SEE
THE EXIT DOOR

(after Keith Haring)

DEAR KEITH:

I'm on Craigslist again. I am angry, ten years ago. And this is Hollywood.

The Casual Encounters ads are scrolling faster than usual; every few minutes a host of two dozen or so repopulate the interface, almost the same rate I am pounding plastic-bottle Gin gimlets, Nina Simone lamenting the whip of Parisian wind amidst the clanging AC of my dilapidated pseudo-Craftsman Hollywood cottage. The hot windless day broke open some rising need—in not only me, it seems; there is a flurry of M4Ms, of the typical photos—hairy chests and waxed chests, dangling and clenched dicks, finger-spread ass-cheeks and slightly parted lips filling the screen with overt sexual demands. I want to feel like a bandit, a punk, a renegade. Like you, Keith.

I first saw your artwork when I signed up for Best Buddies at a community service fair my freshman year in college. Your work was the poster image for the organization: simple faceless figures—one yellow, one orange—arms over shoulder in that classic buddy embrace, against a flat blue backdrop. Best Buddies paired students with mentally disabled adults to go on outings in the community: the zoo, Six Flags. I always took mine—Bobby—to the Krispy Kreme and Kentucky Fried Chicken on Ponce De Leon Avenue in Atlanta. We would take our pink box and family bucket to Piedmont Park and eat it all, lick sugary glaze off fingers and chew cartilage from bone after I got stoned on my cheap eighth of shake. I think we had a good time, me and Bobby. I was probably breaking the Best Buddies rules. I'm sure you would have, too, Keith.

That Best Buddies poster always made me feel, what's the word, jubilant. Perhaps it was the short black lines emanating out from the figures, like vibrations, suggesting movement. Bursting joy? Adolescent jittering? Like ever some kind of possibility. The colors told me: this artist is resolute, satisfied in his bold strokes. Sorry, Keith. I was young.

I thought there was some kind of possibility with a senior at my college, the other tenor in the University Singers chorale, who sat next to me, who tickled me during warm-up, the palest boy you could ever imagine. His thinning hair, the same color as his skin, resembled rough brushstrokes of a monochromatic portrait. He wore ripped jean shorts and no shoes, his feet cleft and mucky. His eyes bulged out, like a Boston Terrier's, lips swollen and cracked like a glazed donut. And I loved him. I even told Bobby about him while I smoked my schwaggy weed in the park, about the time when the senior and I were alone in the auditorium hanging lights for a Christmas concert, and we discussed Judith Butler like we understood it, and he argued that Kinsey was right, and he kissed me and slipped his hands under my shirt, and we went back to his dormroom and I licked his fingers and we cuddled and fell asleep in each other's arms. My first hookup with a boy: a revelation.

Your animal drawings were always my favorite, Keith, especially the dogs, cats and chickens. I am an animal activist, too. Did you know that in order for a chicken to be certified "free-range," all it needs is a minimum of five minutes of access to the outside? At Polyface Farms—a certified "free-range" operation in Virginia—the "outdoors" comprises 5x10-feet fenced-in gravel pits available through a doggie door at the end of the coop, a space to share with no less than 1,000 other chickens.

Most Craigslist ad titles present a litany of raw tingling dangers: Lubed Ass in the Air, Waiting for Stud. I reply with a sepia-toned dick pic. Who Wants Their Cock Drained? Sure! Young Hung Straight Dick for Generous. BBC For Tight Asian Butt. Bear Wants to Train His Cub. I Wanna Drink Your Piss and Jizz. Glory-hole Cum Dump. Fuck Me While I Wear My Girlfriend's Panties. Let Me Lick Your Feet While You Take a Shit on My Mother's Glamour Shot Senior Prom Photograph. That one sounds punk rock. I click it; what do I get? A blurry cock flopped over the waistband of gym shorts. I reply with my body shot, flexing whatever little muscle I have. Another ad entreats, Are There Any Nice Men on Here Anymore? I skip. Cum on My Face? That sounds fun. I repeat with the sepia dick pic. I get a rather truncated response almost immediately: He asks me, "You a top?" I write, "Sometimes." He asks me, "You masculine?" I write, "What does that mean?" He asks me, "Stats?" I write back that I prefer Analytical Geometry. He ceases correspondence.

After my sleepover with the college senior, I spent three weeks worth of nights on the grass of the residential quad, sitting under his dormroom window, waiting until his light went out, hoping he'd glance out the window, spot me under the fluorescence with my face of yearning, that romantic Hollywood someplace-far-away face. But he never did. You see, he never acknowledged that night in his dorm-room, not even when we woke up the next morning, limbs and sweat, a tangled bed. He quietly pulled himself away from the naked embrace while I pretended to sleep, pulled on a pair of sweatpants and began studying at his desk, his broad stretch of back shielding the rest of him from my waking. The back told me that I needed to go, and I slunk out. At the end of chorale practice the next day, I touched his shoulder; he spun and dared me. He whispered through his soft face, "I'm not like you. I want a family." Within 24 hours, he had a girlfriend. I wrote him poetry, would leave it in his mailbox.

I remember a first line of one of the poems: *What does it mean to be like me?*

I remember a last line of one of the poems: *I could love your paradox!*

I once told a guy at the end of a pleasant date that we could only make love for as long as a Nina Simone song. He asked me, "Who is that?" which is when I should have kicked him out. He asked me, "Why should we fuck so quickly?" He asked me, "Are you a top or bottom?" I said, "I like sex to be like a poem." He said, "Poems are too hard to read." He said, "Men aren't supposed to be poetry." He asked me, "Aren't you liberated?" I kicked him out. I sat under my window and wondered if he was right. About the lyrical. About the liberated.

I didn't discover how you really felt about all of this binary bullshit until much later, Keith, when I saw your other images. It wasn't until I saw one in particular, of a headless body being strangled—not at the neck, but at the guts—all muscles and penis against a pink and glitter background—that I knew you were angry, after you had been checked in a bunch of recycled hetero boxes, after you had been rejected by countless lovers as too fem or too butch, too top or too bottom, too one way or the other, one or the other, apron or sledgehammer. How much liberation has there really been that we still liken ourselves to Lucy and Ricky, to Ozzie and Harriet, to high heels and work boots?

Did you know, Keith, that even when the coop door opens for those "free-range" chickens at Polyface—that five-minute opportunity to splay their chicken feet on that wide-open gravel and take in the sunshine— they don't move? You would think they'd ache with the liberation and scuttle towards the door, clucking loudly until that first sliver of light cracks at the bottom of their coop, feathers pouncing in that push to the great big liberty. But, no. The door opens and they sit there, stunned and still, clucking like fools. Even now, after all these years.

I'm angry, Keith. I'm wound, just like your own strangled gut. Liberty is a poly-face.

I am certified now, and this is San Francisco. I have rights. I can even get married. The door has opened and the crack of light is bright and glaring, and I get my five minutes of sunshine. But I want more than the five minutes anyone is offering. I don't want to be a certified free-range faggot. I want to roam the whole fucking farm. I want to wear the boots when I want, the apron when I want, to wield the sledgehammer while scuttling in the highest of heels, but more than that. I want none of it, so I can be *all* of it. I want to splay my feet on the grass of that college quad, only not looking up with a someplace-far-away face, but head-on. A renegade, against a flat, blue backdrop. Because, like you knew, Keith, the only door worth walking through is the one to which you'll never return.

A FICTION MORE REAL

(after *Pink Narcissus*)

A SMOOTH TWINK with an enthusiastic butt crawls nude through a technicolor garden. The sky is dark but the world gleams with a glitter-light, the camera gliding over him, as if the lens has fingers. The twink ponders animatronic butterflies, his nipple with a blade of grass, his self. He stares, kisses his mirrored reflection in a Pepto Bismol boudoir. He tries on different uniforms, different personas: matador, biker, emperor, imp. They become his lovers, his neighbors, his mannequins, his art. And at once, they are all him. A world of delirious fantasy, desire, beauty seen through a kaleidoscope.

James Bidgood filmed almost all of *Pink Narcissus* in his small Chelsea studio over seven years in the sixties. He built the lavish sets himself—crinoline clouds, rivers of lamé, paper flowers. He collected flotsam from costume shops, theatre sets and fabric stores, brought them to his flat like a bird to a nest and fashioned a whole world for this lonely young hustler, played by Bobby Kendall—the soul of Bidgood.

The first network documentary on homosexuality in the United States, aptly titled "The Homosexuals," aired in March 1967 on *CBS Reports* during the middle year of Bidgood's production. Mike Wallace anchored with his guillotine inflection. The episode featured testimony from psychiatrists, cultural critics, lawyers, woven with footage of a dark gay bar and a sex sting operation. Wallace reports to America, "The average homosexual, if there be such, is promiscuous. He is not interested or capable of a lasting relationship like that of a heterosexual marriage. His sex life, his love life, consists of a series of one-chance encounters at the clubs and bars he inhabits. And even on the streets of the city—the pick-up, the one-night stand, these are characteristics of the homosexual relationship."

Because Bidgood's public life consisted of spaces in the dark—bathhouses, porn theatres, silent encounters—perhaps he needed something to be celebrated in bold light. And so he packed his room with fresnels and gels, mirrors and bulbs, to beam the brightness of his mind, a 300 square foot studio in New York City.

In an old college journal of mine, running up the margins, I scribbled *art is the conduit between humanity and the sublime*. I don't remember why I wrote that and wonder if I was stoned when I did. But it stays with me, and I think of that phrase a lot.

Stanley Siegel, in his book *Uncharted Lives*, claims, "Isolation presents a creative world. Sometimes in fantasy we deal with separation by becoming productive—drawing, writing, creating." We express with fantasy in spite of an incomprehensible or hostile reality.

I was seven years old when my mother left home to explore her stolen youth before it entirely disappeared. She was 15 years old when she married my father, who was merely fresh out of high school, himself. They had to travel to South Carolina for the nuptials, the only state that allowed children to marry. Not long after she birthed my older brother, Chris, and my father enlisted in the Marine Corps, did my mother realize her unhappiness. How could she know my father when he wasn't even yet a man? And how could she know herself? Yet my mother tried for years to make it work, like a child of a broken home would do. In all, she lasted seventeen. Imagine a woman of 32 who's already lived a lifetime. She knew there was something more, and needed to find out what it was on her own. The Hawaiian sea breeze whispered this wisdom to her when we'd walk to the shore and stare out at the splice of two-tone blue. I overheard the mutterings myself, and somehow understood what the wind had said, without knowing the exact words.

However, my understanding did not come without pain. Not a sudden wall kind of pain, no. My mother was the center of the world, so when she left the whole middle of my body followed. *And this is how you break a child, you know. Step one, take the mother away.* I retreated, to more than merely my room, escaping however I could the anger, the fighting between Chris and my father, my hand on my stomach, watching it pass right through. I played records, read my *Highlights*, stared at the gaps in my bedroom door and then created, within those eggshell walls, to fill the hole in my belly, a sister: Shenandoah, just like the mountains, the river valley, as sloping and bosomed as the land itself. She had auburn hair that shocked in all directions, a wild bright beauty who traced the cracks of the ceiling with a finger and squinted eye, built forts with bedlinens and books, who kept my secrets. Before sleep, she lying next to me, our foreheads almost touching, I would whisper my biggest secret, "I miss her," and she would whisper back, "She misses you, too."

Shenandoah never left my room, somehow content with the cloistered arrangement. And my loneliness, a self of its own, never questioned her presence. And then, when my father announced he was re-stationed to Quantico, Virginia, a night before we flew across the ocean, Shenandoah slipped through my window, turned back slightly, hair still shrouding her face and ran out into the dark, never to return.

Art is the conduit between humanity and the sublime.

Wallace further reports, "The dilemma of the homosexual: told by the medical profession he is sick; by the law that he's a criminal; shunned by employers; rejected by heterosexual society. Incapable of a fulfilling relationship with a woman, or for that matter a man. At the center of his life he remains anonymous. A displaced person. An outsider."

In high school I told my classmates that I grew up in Tokyo. No, I didn't just tell them I grew up in Tokyo, I lavished upon them an epic tale that could cross an ocean. Even though our Marine Corps family had moved all over the country, and I had traveled more than most my age, I fabricated an even more exuberant history. My classmates were perceptive enough to know I was different—which inspired in me a new isolation—and were too consumed with their own belonging to complicate matters by including me. I was not legible to them, so I made myself the most extraordinary thing to read, a flashy billboard. I could describe for them Tokyo's skyline, the neon lights, onigiri vendors perched in front of my residential high-rise, a kaleidoscope of place, though I'd never stepped foot on Honshu. I decorated this history with layered backdrops, vivid stories, images and characters as tactile as fabric, a complete world of my own, and presented to them this cinema, of sorts. I saw it, then, as a gift, somehow, not a deception, and certainly not what it truly was.

I would perform often these fabrications—these deceptions—throughout my youth. Stories of exotic travel, of chance encounters with love, stories of my body, perhaps all desires made manifest, tinged with a rolling language that drew people near. Which desire held me most? Their proximity, or mine?

Art is the conduit between humanity and the sublime.

Towards the end of *Pink Narcissus*, after a street sequence outside of the twink hustler's flat, where throngs of vendors hawk butt-plugs and blowjobs, there is a fourth wall crack in the camera lens, and a deep Russian swell in the score that sobers the delirium. Bidgood suggests the twink's fabricated world turns tawdry once it leaves the asylum of his room. This room, his mind. We realize how necessary that lens had been, now that it is broken. Man is born beautiful, but everywhere outside his mind is degraded. That is our hostile reality.

Once my yarns of Tokyo were discovered as lies, they lost all their intrinsic beauty, this lustrous imagery cracked. My schoolmates flipped from arms-length awe to anger with a torrent I never escaped. Why they seethed, of course, I shamefully understand. I never called what I was doing art. And without a lens that could be cracked, it is presumed by others to be truth, and truth of a different kind than it is—and was—for me.

Soon I was to fathom my imprudence, and upon so withdrew into art. I opened the room of my imagination wide—the doors, the windows, the closet—with a pen instead of my tongue, and endowed fantasies that could not be confused with lies. And yet, these fictions told only a kind of truth, certainly not what it truly was. You move a vase from one side of the room to the other, and there is a change, a sense, a new reality to the thing.

Shenandoah appears in my dreams often. Her hair spills over my shoulder as we read a book together, or we run along the walls of my room that are probably smaller than I remember. She is not a memory, more a truth than true, imagination made material. A fiction more real than most of my lived reality.

A couple of years ago I was visiting a friend in Chelsea. I discovered that she lived directly below James Bidgood, in the same building where it all happened. I imagined the flotsam floating in every crevice, in every corner of his imagination made material, that small studio above my head. The layered history in my mind's eye made my elbows tingle. She asked me, "You want to meet him, see the apartment?" I did. I really did. I wanted to meet the man who remained anonymous until only 15 years ago, with this soufflé of a film. I wanted to hold one of the animatronic butterflies, run the lamé along my forefinger, and breathe on the very mirror that Bobby Kendall pressed his lips to 50 years before. But even as my heart leapt, I shook my head, slowly, and said to her, "That's okay."

I wanted to tell her that some things need to remain one's fantasy. I wanted to tell her that if I went into that room, the nameless twink and his imaginings might slip out the window and never return.

THE MODERN PROMETHEUS, REPRISE

(after Mary Shelley's *Frankenstein,* and various film adaptations)

I.

THE STORY OF FRANKENSTEIN is about a man and a monster. Man, shaped of clay, given fire. Monster, Man's puerile harness of that fire, an ugly shape. A metaphor that makes us: man and monster, lover and lyre, alchemy's folly, these thievings of fire.

This is what I told myself: all geniuses are broken children. A motherless boy bears the void, hardens desire, and chooses science: gives his entirety to what his grief believes. His clay self a bisque in the world while his soft stuff stays with its want; and within the wet center he whimpers. And from that, the brutal imagination.

Imagine the lightning. Plasma, forked and white against rain, the darker of nights. There is a lab coat, a stone floor. The scientist summons— no, that can't be. The scientist conjures—no, that can't be. The scientist *waits*, for the kiss of cloud to ground, a cathode crack in the indigo folds of cockcrow, and then the spark of life, more instinct than imagination. More meat than mind.

II.

You had such a hope in me, that I would kiss your cloud. I saw it in the way you crossed your feet when we argued. I saw it when you tried to parallel my steps when we walked. And the knowing of what failed was there, betrayed in the sight and the step. I'd blink, you'd blink. We would take the same picture, but always off by a breath, by our small hesitations.

There would be a dusk. You would stare into the falling sun, because you knew it was foolish, a disregard of body for beauty: the maker heart, the most adored of fools. You knew this, and I adored you, not because of this; you also loved the light, how it glinted your eyes, made you a different color. You would stare at the sun to find what you wanted in me, the blown shine smoothing my delineations, until there was only an open field for you to run through.

III.

The story of Frankenstein is about a man and what he makes. The child hides behind a curtain and whispers instructions. Let's imagine, as you often do: on a slab, the scientist shaping matter, skin and bone, blood and coil, hand sculpting organ, heart, liver, lymph. Do details matter? He sees what he wants. He stares into the horror and sees a man, sees his mother, sees a promise, then another. And waits for lightning.

I told you that the story of Frankenstein was about a man who created a monster, and you said no it's not, it's about the monster himself, and I said that is a common misconception, and you said the commons were the people's progress, and I said I bet you didn't read the book, and you didn't say anything, and I said you just saw the Karloff movie, I bet, and you said that proves nothing. I didn't say anything. You said don't look at me that way. You said I was a misconception. You said there is truth in the skin of things.

Doesn't it only make sense that lightning would be the fire of life? Something to harness, the lust of it, something so unyielding, so violent. So not of bone, so not of clay.

IV.

Your hope was all around me, enveloping, manic, and I could have crushed you. The knees you made for me did not bend. The head you found for me did not bow. The heart you pressed did not beat your rhythm. I was afraid. You made me too big and I couldn't fit in the world. My hands squeezed, my feet thudded, my words stomped. I hurt everything, the soft stuff around you. I could not live as what you imagined; it was all large, and no multitude.

V.

The story of Frankenstein is about a man and what he mistakes. Isn't it strange that in some movie incarnations the monster kills his creator— isn't it a strange choice? Victor moves in to embrace the wretch, the skinned Adam of his labors (because we need to touch what we make, no matter how foul its form). And after its treachery, its plasma fury, its killing heart, killed, Victor leans into the mass, and a trust of no reason envelops him, and the creature envelops him, wraps giant arms, creation wrapping arms around creator (because don't we want the things we make to be bigger than ourselves?). And pulls the scientist into the experiment, snaps his bones, beaker glass beneath the weight of anxious fingers, that large hand to cowl, or small of back, the places where we fold easy. Isn't it a strange choice? Please know why I ask this.

Don't we all believe to bear it away? Don't we all stare into our want, relentlessly? Don't we all know the grief that burns a cottage to the ground?

I didn't want to be your monster. I didn't want the story of Frankenstein to be about you. But what is a story without want, anyway?

LOVE, IN 7 (OR, LOOK SOMEONE IN THE EYE AS YOU DENY THEM)
(after Mickalene Thomas' *Maya #7*)

1. EYES/LOS ANGELES, CALIFORNIA. After the fireworks on the 4th of July. We lie in bed, our bodies forked, wooden clothespins on a laundry line. We stare at the popcorn ceiling of the room crafted with our felt and glue-gun fantasies. You say, "I don't know what I will be after you." I say, "We are all a composite of places and people." You say, "But so much of who I am is because of you." I say, "That will change." You say, "I don't believe you." I don't say anything. I want to believe that you don't believe me. I want to believe that I will always be the biggest piece of you, the central story. I want to believe the story hasn't ended yet. But I know that you will leave tomorrow. I know that you are bright and beautiful and will meet many places and people. I think at that moment of the time we went jumping off the Bridge to Nowhere, how glittered your eyes were, how grateful. I remember when you begged me to jump a second time. I think of that moment, and now woefully regret that I didn't. It is now as dark as a night in Los Angeles will ever be. You hold my hand and say through tears, "I'm scared." I softly squeeze yours, thinking I know what you're scared of, but I am wrong.

2. Couch/Asheville, North Carolina. You drive up from Atlanta to see how I am settling in. The almost empty farmhouse is a slate gray with a porch that faces bramble. I take you to a Meat and Three and marvel how they get the greens right—just enough bitter, just enough sweet. I walk you to the

French Broad and presto my hands, *This is a real river, not the toxic trickle of the Chattahootchie*. You humble your mouth and remain small, keeping your step beside me, holding your breath so that your fingers brush mine like a feather. I wave my hands like I'm selling the city. Once we get back to the farmhouse, you sit down on the blue Natuzzi couch that last week I hauled out of your suburban Atlanta flat, and you softly pat the space next to you and smile. I turn and say, "I have to unpack." And you knew I meant, "I have to go."

3. Hair/Kailua, Hawai'i. You arrive on the doorstep of the house you used to live in—that we lived in together—with a puppy that smells like bread and sausage. You know I will be excited, and I am, but not exactly for what you think. I hold the puppy and tell you about all the things that I only told you about when you were always there, and the litany has you laugh. But I wasn't done yet. You ask me to come up with a name for the dog. I choose Cinnamon because he is sweet and brown, and then I ask where you live now. You don't answer. I ask you if you are staying for dinner. You don't answer. I ask other questions I care nothing about, just to keep you longer, but you know what I'm doing, and you tell me you love me. I know you love me, Mama, which is why the dog hurts me somehow. When you leave, I don't follow you to the door, because Cinnamon is now mine and I have to take care of him. To me, that means to hold him in my arms and never let him go. But I watch you walk out, and the last I see of you through the closing door is your beautiful red hair hiding your face as you pull it closed. Two weeks later, Cinnamon will escape that same door and run directly under a neighbor's tire.

4. Wall/Seattle, Washington. We are sun-burning on a boat in Lake Union, you and I and a guy you like and our girlfriend that he likes. We jump into the water and pull ourselves out and lay on the deck and consider our bodies that approach middle-age and yet feel youthful to us still. You arrange your golden hair in front of your bikini, mermaid-style. "I wish we all lived in

the same city," you say. "Why don't you all move up here." I say, "I love the Bay. It feels like home. But it's fun to visit you." You fall silent, and turn your head west, because it's easy to hide the truth when the sun dowses your face. Our friends are splashing each other, and I laugh at their flirtation. You want to tell me that you feel alone here, and I know this, but you don't say it. So, I scooch my body closer to you—not to be closer, but to show it—and I make a goofy face at you, the same one that has eased you for 15 years. Your eyes betray the bittersweet-ness that I know you feel, but you smile anyway. I place my hand on yours. I want to tell you that I can't be everything you need, and you know this, which is why you say nothing more and allow the sun to hide this hurting.

5. Hands/Memphis, Tennessee. I've known you only for ten minutes and you've already asked me to be your friend. We are sitting in an empty bar drinking Abitas—you here because you like the people, I here because it was the closest bar off the highway exit, the highway I'm driving all the way to California. I tell you I started the day in Asheville, and you wish you've been there. You have such a kind face, and your shoulders are easy and wide. You say, "Let's go on an adventure," and you drive us to a small shotgun house and score some ecstacy. We drop and walk through the city. You stop and say, "Before we blow up, I want you to know that I'm doing this with you because I feel a connection." I nod slowly, and we continue walking. We weave in and out of neighborhoods in the night, we dance in a blues bar that smells like urine and Hubba Bubba. When the still dark sky begins to open for morning, we grab our guitars and play badly on the banks of the Mississippi next to a bridge that goes nowhere. You are so happy there are tears in your eyes, and you say, "It's easy to be close to you," and you place your hand on my chest. You then feel my heart beat faster and understand. Our bodies wasted, you invite me to rest back at your flat. Your girlfriend greets me with a sleepy smile at the door, and we all collapse on your bed, beyond exhausted. You whisper in her ear, and then begin to kiss her, running your hands through her hair. I turn my back to you, and as I

do, you touch my back and say, "Stay. You can watch." Your hand is the perfect warmth, but I want to knock it away. You think you are giving me something, your eyes beaming. I rise from the bed and leave the room. The two of you already return to passion as I close the front door and face the morning. I drive nonstop to Oklahoma City.

6. Window/Baltimore, Maryland. We are watching the light fade behind the loading cranes on the harbor. Mama is surfing the internet inside the house while we drink sweet tea on the back porch. It's a bit cold, but we like the temporary separation, we like that it is just us brothers. You say, "It's nice to be together as a family." I nod and stare out at the water in the far distance, because I never know what you really mean when you say things. You talk about how good your work is going, how grown your girls have become. Things are looking up for you. Then you say that things would be even better if you just had a couple thousand dollars to keep you in the black, that times are tough: school supplies, rent, food on the table kind of times. I think about the summer you stole my car. I think about the spring you promised you'd use the money to check into rehab. I think about the winter you wept into the phone and said your daughter had leukemia. I think about everything that comes out of your mouth and how it swirls into a thing that makes me shake. I think about how much I've always wanted to believe you. I look squarely at your wrinkled brow and say, only, "No," my eyes fixed as I sip my tea, my breath a small cloud of ice. I don't shiver, but I shake. Your wounded mouth almost makes me say sorry, but I reconsider—I know now that would only hurt you more. I have learned to look someone in the eye as I deny them.

7. Mouth/Rapid City, South Dakota. We have driven miles through corn fields, listening to podcasts and pop tunes and our five-year plans. My hand is on your thigh, as it always is when you drive, and I keep motioning you to quit biting the skin around your nails. We hiked through the Badlands earlier that morning and you ask me why all the beautiful corners of America

are so redneck. I say it has more to do with proximity than beauty, and you say proximity to nothing, and I say don't make statements in the form of questions, that it's sardonic, and I slap your thigh and laugh. You make that sound deep in your throat when you're thoroughly pleased. I look at you while you drive, so content, and I think I have done something right for a change. We are driving cross country and I feel I am showing you a world that is somehow mine but that now will be somehow yours. I marvel how after all these years there is still something new for us to share. And all this makes my hand on your thigh hot, and I notice the rest of your leg in the heat, and then more of you. And I can only think that I want my mouth on you, that I want to take you in more and more until I realize I can't get enough. But when I lean down to make this a gift, you kick your leg up and hit my chin. I look up at you in shock, and you laugh and say, "I'm driving." But the laugh is not playful. It is borne of anger, or something proximal. I pull back and rub away at my chin, not because it hurts. I say, "Look at me when you do that." A small cloud of ice escapes my mouth. You stone your face forward, and I watch the color fade from your lips faster than any escape. The lines of the road run into our dashboard, and the rhythm of silence that always makes its way finds a pulse. I look over to you, and know that you are more hurt than I, and that is what makes my blood warm back and quicken. I place my hand on your thigh again, and you, without hesitation, without so much as a shiver, slide your fingers in mine like you were made of butter, and I watch your face return to its full, brown, open love. And once again, I flood with the feeling that I have done something right for a change.

THE 15ᵀᴴ ROCK

(after the kare-sansui garden in the Temple of Ryōan-ji, Kyoto)

I WAS BORN on the Summer Solstice in the Year of the Dragon. I knew growing up that the Solstice was the longest day of the year, associated with power and creativity, but I wasn't familiar with the Chinese zodiac until my mother's empath friend, Margaret, widened her eyes upon learning my birthdate. "Oh my."

"A fire dragon and the first crab in Solstice. Fire and water. You'll cook up some powerful stuff. Just make sure you always have a pot on the stove, or there will be a big mess."

I am in Kyoto, Japan, the temple of Ryōan-ji. I am sitting on the veranda of the hojo, viewing the famous dry landscape garden on the temple grounds, tourists wandering around sneaking pictures. The white gravel is meticulously raked in lines traversing the length of the garden, with circles rippling out from the rocks placed asymmetrically in the rectangular space. I am alone.

I read in my guidebook that there are fifteen stones arranged in the garden, but the stones are placed so that the entire composition cannot be seen at once. In fact, from any angle on the veranda one can exactly and only see 14 rocks. It is understood that only through enlightenment one would be able to view the 15ᵗʰ rock.

I desired enlightenment. I traveled a great distance for it. I came to Japan sadder than I had ever been. To see the 15ᵗʰ rock would have made me feel purposeful, or at least given me validation that I was not altogether a monster.

I came to Japan because I made a mess. I was a liar. I had just turned 21, and the throng of friends I surrounded myself with those first years of college had dwindled to a sympathetic handful, and those few were gone for the summer. Instead of sitting alone in my crappy apartment complex colloquially referred to as Peachtree Garbage, I applied for traveling fellowships on FastWeb, this one a week-long immersion trip through a Japanese-American cultural exchange.

I chose Japan, perhaps, because it was one of the first lies I remember telling. In high school, I wove a rich, detailed life history prior to attending Cardinal Gibbons to compel the cliquish boys at the school, and particularly Chris, whom I thought the most beautiful person in the world. The lies shimmied like fringe: I had hung out with Prince backstage at a concert, I was a child of nomadic hippies, and—included in that skein—I had lived for a glorious year near the Emperor's Palace in Tokyo. Of course, my classmates had figured me out, eventually, but if it weren't for Chris' pained glare of my betrayal, I would have dismissed them all without feeling an inkling of regret. In other words, I didn't learn my lesson then.

I come back to the Ryōan-ji garden the next day, determined to find a vantage that would give me sight of the 15th rock. I need catharsis, a signifier of growth, something literary or cinematic, something that makes a bell ring in the chamber of my resolve. And, like a Western fool, I hunt for it, I turn outward, Manifest Destiny. Remember, I am 21. I scooch from one end of the veranda to the other in waist-wide increments, sit, and count. 14. I scooch again. 14. All the way across. I notice that all 15 rocks can be identified in a combination of vantages, but only 14 from any given view.

I didn't lie to elevate impressions, to draw people to me. I lied because I was afraid people would leave. The lies would only begin once we grew close. That's why my lies were more potent. You can imagine how hurtful it must have been, to be lied to even after you have come to love a person. It makes the fall that much farther, and the ground that much harder.

I was alone in Japan just as I was turning 21 because I had fallen far, the farthest I had ever fallen. Just before the semester ended, an anonymous flyer circulated around the Academic Quad buildings of our tiny liberal arts college. It was entitled "The Pathological Liar." It didn't name me explicitly, but being such a small campus, many students—and certainly I—could figure it out. The flyer was a scathing confession as if written by me, listing things I had said. Some were exaggerated recounts, but many were spot-on lies I indeed had told: that I had been in a punk band in high school, that I had traveled cross-country in a VW bus before I came to college. Most sobering in this faux confession were the things I had confided with vulnerability that were actually true: that my brother was a genius who had fallen into drug and alcohol abuse, that I had been assaulted on a military base as a kid. A student whom I had been friends with compassionately collected and disposed of the flyers as fast as he could (thank you, Jeremy), but the damage was done. I couldn't walk anywhere on campus without feeling the burning glare of ridicule or, even worse, of betrayal. I even received sneers, some from students I barely knew. I clutched my books tight and kept my head down. When folks use the phrase "my world came crashing down on me" I understand the accuracy of the platitude. In the tight bubble of Oglethorpe University's social orbit, my world felt collapsed, and gravity pulled me down until I was kissing the ground. I had made a big mess.

Because here's the thing: I was a loving person. An empathic, deeply feeling person. I lived in the intuitive rhythm of the world, my soul a big open thing. That is what rendered the betrayal that much more painful to those who decided to love me back. I can imagine them questioning if *any* of the friendship was true, in the wake of my dishonesty. And that's what hurt me most, that those people I loved felt betrayed. And, I had no one to blame but myself.

And so, I am in Japan, in Kyoto, on the veranda of Ryōan-ji, looking for that 15th fucking rock. And I fail. I peer from every inch of that veranda and always—only—14 rocks. I am alone. I go to Tokyo. I drink tea, I eat lots of food with mayonnaise on it. I buy Kirins from vending machines. I walk the streets near the Emperor's Palace, which look nothing like my vividly detailed accounts to Baltimore high school jocks five years before. The regret lowers itself in a bucket until it sinks beyond my vision. A stone settles in the deep recesses of my gut. The weight has me glean some kind of understanding with my *Stranger in a Strange Land* scenario, and I return to Georgia feeling I have grokked something.

And I did, sort of. I realized I needed to stop lying. But that was like cutting the tail off a salamander.

Another five years later, I fell in love, with Aram. While in the relationship, there was nurturing, there was kindness, openness and trust. We communicated where our hearts were while we strolled through our neighborhood, when we made love in a tent filling with thunderstorm rain while camping in the Ozarks, on postcards we'd write to one another. When I spoke, there was a clear, direct language to his heart. Aram fell in love with the best version of myself I had ever been. I felt certain of the love, and possessed no fear of abandonment. But when it ended unexpectedly, that fear gurgled up like magma in a rock belly, and I erupted deception that shot up and out, and it went everywhere. I was that ex you roll your eyes about over stories in loud bars with sugary drinks. I slipped into Aram's account, read his emails and then made up lies that somehow attempted to evoke serendipity, curating a destiny that brought us back together. I'd show up at a concert he was attending, and then act surprised when I ran into him. I'd drop mention of places he had just discovered in casual texts. I even bought *Phantom of the Opera* tickets adjacent to his seats, despite me hating that musical. "Oh, Aram! How strange that we are sitting right next to each other!" This was also the beginnings of social media, and I can claim to be a true pioneer of catfishing. With this new Facebook application, I created a persona, Seamus—ruddy, black-Irish kind of handsome—that befriended Aram, that was "dating" me. Seamus would "confess" to Aram that I wasn't over him, that I talked about Aram all the time, ad nauseum infinitum. To make it seem realistic, Seamus even friended many of my other friends, having separate conversations with them, all while he tried to convince Aram that he and I were meant to be together. I was so hellbent on winning Aram back with this complex tangle that I didn't even consider the dishonesty of it all.

And when it all came out that Seamus was my creation, that I had lied to my friends, to Aram, a world that I thought I was shouldering pretty well those last few years, crashed down on me again.

But this time it was even harder, because I had betrayed myself. Something I thought was part of my past not only resurfaced, but did so without me even recognizing it before I had wound such a cloverleaf of deceit. That not only humiliated me, it scared me. What else was I capable of doing?

Chastened and unwell, I moved out of my house in the Highland Park neighborhood of Los Angeles to stay with my friend Dana in her cloistered Los Feliz bungalow. She had an extra room available that summer, and offered it to me until I recuperated. I decided, instead, to reside on the couch on her front porch. I didn't tell her this then, but I felt unworthy to fully accept such an open-handed and civil offer as a bedroom. The four walls seemed too generous.

During this convalescence, I laid on that couch for hours a day, staring at the trees that surrounded Dana's bungalow, counting the leaves of the magnolia branch that hung close to the eave of the house. I read pages from a book, then I stared out from the small world of the porch. Read, and stared.

It was this time on Dana's porch that I came to realize that I often curated my life, tried to arrange it for maximum effect, especially in an effort to keep those I loved from ever leaving, but in that rigorous effort I forgot that I was part of the arrangement, too. I can't tell you the exact moment I realized this—what I was reading or what inspired me to think in this way, particularly—but I know I was on that soft, ratty couch, surrounded by the trees, my books and hopelessness. And this, dear reader, was a true, honest-to-Goddess catharsis, almost cinematic in its impact. My mind traveled back to Kyoto, to Ryōan-ji. I was the 15th rock. *I* was the 15th rock.

And if we are all the world's 15th rock, we must be what we want the world to be. That is the arrangement. It is so embarrassingly simple, to share it in writing, here, in this essay. Yet, no realization has impacted me with that sort of velocity since. It was a bona fide grokking.

Soon after the couch catharsis, Irwan and I found a cottage of our own in the heart of Hollywood. Soon after that, I would begin teaching Visual Culture at an art school, and my new life would commence. This new life would less and less feel the fear of abandonment, because I understood that to feel abandoned is to not recognize oneself as an intrinsic part of the world. There is no abandonment. There is leaving, but even that is merely moving along the same plane in a different direction. I am as much as everything else, an interconnected arrangement, a single curation with infinite forms. I must be what I want the world to be. What a thing to recognize. I had much to become.

One of the first lessons of my Visual Culture course involves the kare-sansui garden at the Ryōan-ji Temple. I show a map of Japan, pictures of Kyoto, the temple, then the garden itself, its white gravel and mossy stones. I begin the lesson with a simple fact: Ryōan-ji means "dragon at peace."

ALIGNMENT

WE HUDDLE TOGETHER on the backyard picnic bench. The trees are naked and knobbed. The light is snuffed, but it makes our colors pull forward. Among the bundle, there is ease. One couple leans together, one does not. The faces are not laughing, or glamming for the camera, but are soft in their smiles, at rest, at ease. At trust, in love, a kindness for what they look at. They are looking at the photographer. My mother.

This photo hangs on the stairwell wall of my Victorian flat in San Francisco, a wall of images my husband arranged, his careful creation—his Ikibana to my dancing lotus—that gives everyone a punch of joy upon walking in our home. This photo is New Years 2006, my mother's house in Baltimore. My heart has finally healed from a certain love that taught me a new truth of love, and I wanted to celebrate the lesson with those I loved before. We come from all over: Atlanta, Los Angeles, Seattle, New Jersey. I wanted to reintroduce myself to the world. There's only one word for love.

The afternoon winter light is bleak in Baltimore, a murky gray, a cold brown. The clang of loading barges in the harbor, metal on rusted metal, floating atop metallic water, the walls of brick, the color of rust. The perfect word for a color, a feeling. If any of us possessed that feeling here—which we do not—it would be for our future selves. One will play hypocrite and betray his wife. One will fall paranoid to danger and disappear to West Virginia. One will declare betrayal by the whole world. One will be dying and not know it. But for now, our steel is gleaming, our shine is good. There will be rusting soon, but for now we are blemish free.

Before we sat on this bench, before we hailed the fortune of our orbital alignment, we chased Kobe, my mother's white Shiba Inu, through the eternally rusting neighborhood. It was a Benny Hill skit, a yakety saxophone, all of us running willy-nilly, flailing arms and scampering legs. After an hour, Christian saved the day, and as we dragged Kobe home, I asked him, "Do you love Stephanie." And he said, "Yes." And I said, "I'll kill you if you hurt her." And he said, "I won't," and laughed. I laughed too, but I meant it. My eyes welled with the surprise of how much I meant it. I wondered what that was, this loyalty. I had just healed from my own hurting heart, and the healing was the best part of all. Why feel the need to protect one from this possibility, when that possibility makes for wisdom? I guess a kind of love. A myopic love. We say such stupid things when peering into the future.

The night before, in the basement of my mother's house, we drank whiskey and played Never Ever Have I Ever. Such a dangerous game to play with your mother in the room, especially amongst people who know all of your transgressions. Irwan cornered me with details that had me admit to anonymous sex in a car, to drugs and rocking my roll. We prompted each other with stories we all knew, that we often helped write but wanted to hear again, a lived sound in an open space. We humiliated one another with a kindness only time and trust can bring—familiar tears and aching bellies. A game is always danger with so many people in a room, but I was grateful to practice the honesty.

The year before was a time of healing. Not only for the heartbreak, but for the hearts I broke. You see, whenever pain gripped me, my imagination spun out of control, and I crafted stories that I presented as truth, largely because I believed them. Whole histories in places I've never been, people that never existed. Pathology is a word that comes to mind. It was never to deceive, but somehow something to give while I disappeared, like the weaving of a dazzling fabric under which to hide. I wove lies that I thought would pad me on all sides. The breakup with Aram spurred such a time, and I went wild with the world in my mind.

I had to face it. The year before this New Years was that time, and though it was the hardest thing I'd ever done, I emerged grateful for what I had owned. I was now taking steps to commit all the lies to paper before they escaped my mouth so they could be something useful, something closer to truth.

Before this photo, I thought I'd need to start over, start from scratch, that no one could love a man who loved them while lying. But what was true about me was how much I loved. The truth of me was more than the sum of the stories I told. And this motley bundle knew this. They forgave me before I conceded a single transgression.

Years later, Adrian will cheat on Katie after endlessly tormenting her with his own unfounded and cloying jealousy. I will fly Katie out to San Francisco, and we will walk. I will remember this New Years, how all of us worried over the pathetic skein of his wants. Katie and I will walk for days, and not much else, because that's what she wants.

My mother takes this photograph, her gift for our presence. I assemble those I love to meet me at my mother's house to share in my repair, always an invention. Katie and I are in the kitchen making pasta. The others, in the basement, reminiscing their shared past. I cup her shoulder and tell her how sorry I am for mine. She rolls and smiles her very Irish eyes: "Everyone sucks sometimes, Miah," she says. "Everyone hurts."

LIFE ON MARS

(after David Bowie)

YOU STAND IN A SPACE, a no space, gleaming white background light. You wear a powder blue suit, so long on the thin of you, as if your limbs were mere piping for the hang of fabric. Royal blue eyeshadow pales against your flat gray eyes, orange rocker mullet, pink lips.

"He looks like a girl," my father says. I am inches from the cathode tube of our MTV in the living room of our ranch-styled duplex in the center of Kane'ohe Bay Naval base, Hawai'i, my father's Marine Corps biceps repetitively flexing in the reflection of the screen as he lifts the dumb-weights of his ego. "Must be gay," my father says behind me, his forearm rising and falling like a breathing machine, like a machine, like a non-breathing machine.

I can't quit staring at the video. Simple, no story, you in makeup. You sing directly into the camera. You face me. And I know, somehow, this is not about you looking like a girl. It's about something bigger. I am seven years old.

You made the video to "Life on Mars" in the mid-70s, when your alter ego Ziggy folded into your entire self, where only corners of Davie Jones were peeling away from the celluloid. This was your most prolific time, full of concert tours and cocaine, of simulating fellatio with Ronson's guitar and songs of capitalist exhaustion. Of course, I may not have known most of this at seven years old, but what I did know was that you were mine, one of my tribe, even though I didn't know what that meant.

I didn't know this until much later, but you began writing your life story on the very day my life began.

Before Prince, before Siouxsie Sioux, before funk singer Betty Davis, was you. My first icon. Idol. While God demanded we make no images in the likeness of the divine, I wanted to paint myself into Ziggy, lightning bolted and spikey, neon and ghost. I would align my face with yours on the screen, match our delineations, our features, until my eyes blurred from the bright knowledge.

I didn't know this until much later, but you once told the press that "Los Angeles should be wiped off the face of the Earth."

My time of knowing was that in-between, after the nude be-ins and before the real revolution began, before metrosexual and genderfluid, before trans and queer. There was man, there was woman. There was gay, there was straight. There was baseball and baking. And then, there was you. An in-between. A nothing in particular, and yet a glimmer of all those things. I felt safer in the nowhere space, that ambiguity. I didn't color within the lines. Never danced to the steps. I looked across the flat concrete military base horizon and knew that you were precisely on the other side of this round planet, that if I dug below my feet long enough, the tunnel would be the spine of our world.

I was certain we were part of the same whole. You were a dancer. You loved *commedia*, the harlequin. You lived for funk records, said you "heard God" when you listened to Little Richard. Your mother's name was Peggy. I mentioned this to my Peggy. She said, "He is a really good musician." She said, "He knows a lot about outer space." She said, "He is a bit weird, though." And she ran her fingers in my auburn mop and winked a wink that could be seen across a galaxy.

I didn't know this until much later, but you were a fairy-taled Tin Man, pushed by a bulldozer. To where? You never let us know. *Ashes to ashes, funk to funky.* I have felt the metallic chase of that machine for so long. I guess neither of us knew where it would end us up.

My second-grade class portraits. My mother dressed me in a white Oxford and black slacks and a smooth cowlick. She sent me off "spiffy," as she would say. But I knew you would never allow the camera to capture you in something so boxed, so buttoned. When I arrived to school, I pulled out the sleeveless mesh top with a royal blue bolt across the chest that my friend Amanda found at a yard sale. I ran water through my auburn mop and pulled it to the sky. I walked to the flashing bulb and faux forest backdrop with "Fame" pulsing in my blood-beat head. Snap. When the pictures came in the mail, my mother was amused, my father was harumph, and the last word from his lips that night was "gay." At least, that is what I remember being the last word, even if there were more. He had called *you* that once. But I knew you were bigger than that. And that meant I was bigger than that, too, somehow.

When I first moved to Los Angeles for grad school, I called my mother and said, "Peggy, this fucking place should be wiped off the face of the Earth." She winked through the phone.

When my father emerged from a ten-year absent tenure, lifting the dumb-weights of his bulldozed ego—never creative enough as you to alter one—I realized I was face to face with a man who could sell the world. And when he extended his hand kindly—he indeed was kind, but to be good you need to be more than that—my own olive branch hidden behind my back, I sang to him, *I thought you died alone, a long long time ago.*

I didn't know this until much later, but I was strong. That is why my father stayed away. That is why my mother winked at me. Strength is a thing summoned, to face what comes. My father could not look me in the eye. I was a thing to face. I wish I had known that, then. But I didn't read Virginia Woolf's letter to Leonard until twenty-two: *To look life in the face, always, to look life in the face, and to know it for what it is...at last, to love it for what it is, and then, to put it away.* I guess that is why I write this essay. To love my father for what he is. That is the strength I give to him, to me. And then I put it away, accept it into the rest of whatever time is left. *Tomorrow belongs to those who can hear it coming.*

I guess that means we weren't exactly the same after all, you and I. I remain surprised that you didn't face the end the way Ziggy would: head on, electric one-liners, not knowing where you're going, but assuring it wouldn't be boring. But that doesn't mean I am drawn to you any less. And perhaps there is a strength in your final silence that I have yet to understand, and will one day. No matter. You gave me some bright knowledge. And I will forever be grateful.

Our history is a lightning bolt first across the chest, and then across a field, and then a continent. I never saw you live, and life has traveled far, but you've lived in me all this time. And when you *strung out in heaven's high* I thought *I had hit an all-time low*. But that was brief, this sigh one must release for a star man, the necessary wailing grief of a changed fairy-taled world. I knew the heart of you was here, within your thin white duke, within your tin machine. It echoed in the cathedral of my memory—as a child, dancing, as an adult, dancing. Your gleaming white background light, and now this time you the one winking, as you sang,

Let the children lose it. Let the children use it. Let all the children boogie.

DEAR ANTONIO SABATO, JR.

(after those hot 90s Calvin Klein underwear ads)

DEAR TONY,

I find it ironic that I am writing this particular letter to you, this letter in 2019, considering it's not the first time I have felt the need to evince to you in the form of written correspondence. You see, I wanted to write you almost thirty years ago for inspiring in me my first media-assisted orgasm, that Calvin Klein underwear ad in the perfumed pages of *Rolling Stone*. You were staring directly at me, sitting on a stool in white thigh-huggers, your legs spread like an invitation for a margarine party. And you were saying to me: "Go ahead, little man. Touch it. Think of my waistband as possibility." And I did, believe me, as regularly as brushing my teeth. My flummoxed mama once asked me, noticing the molested condition of that September 1990 magazine cover, "You like MC Hammer that much?" followed by, "Ow. Why does the carpet in your room cut my feet?"

But I'm not writing to say thanks for those lip-twisting eruptions that you summoned from my pre-teen volcano body, nor for how the land-mass of my bedroom floor forever altered its geology due to your smoldering and insistent solicitation. Nor am I sharing with you how many times I watched Janet Jackson's "Love Will Never Do Without You" video, just to get a glimpse of you and Djimon Hounsou rollicking black-and-white on a deserted beach, me forever harboring resentment for her selfish man-hoarding.

You killed it, Antonio! Your gleaming teeth and rounded shoulders and I've-got-a-secret smile and the-secret-is-that-my-dick-is-from-Sicily underwear bulge could have forever been branded in my memory as ideal beauty in only the way that an adolescent first guarantees. Sure, I've seen more beautiful men in the years since—Gael Garcia Bernal, Taye Diggs, Brad Pitt in *Fight Club*, not to mention the moment I fully lost control of my body in the movie theatre and reflexively knuckled my husband upon sight of Michael B. Jordan's shirtless entrance in that *Black Panther* fight scene. But you were the first! *You!* No matter what I witnessed in my adulthood, you would have certainly been the eclipsing figure in my erotic death-bed life-montage (directed by Lars von Trier, of course).

But you ruined everything. On June 6th, 2018, you clinched 2nd place in the race for a congressional seat to represent Ventura County for the Republican Party. Granted, being a politician alone is a buzzkill, but that isn't what ruined it for me. After all, I wanked it a few times to Obama's 2014 State of the Union Address, and maybe once to the portrait of a young Rutherford B. Hayes.

But it's what you have *said*, Antonio:

Here is you, on immigration: "I support a wall.... There should be no shortcuts for those who don't want to pay or wait. Refugees should have thought to begin the process sooner."

Boner Killer.

Here is you, on religion: "If Obama's not a Muslim, we should call him President Barry. His name isn't Christian! He changed his name to Barack because he is a Muslim."

Dick Shrinker.

Here is you, on oppression: "After I began supporting Trump, I was blacklisted from Hollywood. I was mocked on Twitter. I feel like a Jew during the Holocaust."

No Feeling Left in the Entire Penile Area, Whatsoever.

So, you see, you have now ruined this sexual mythology of my youth. And that is why I write to you. There are few things left that are sacred in this age of tweeted populism and smartphone exposés. Myth and mystery are disappearing faster than complex discourse. And without either, we become an alphabet soup of denotations and flat symbology, a culture full of politics and a culture empty of poetry. I was already worried about this. And now, you.

But don't worry, Antonio. I might be crestfallen by your betrayal, but I'm not broken. None of us are. We still have our imaginations, no matter the molested condition of your own. So guess what I'm going to do? I'm going to waltz into my bedroom, open my laptop, and stream *Black Panther* on a bright afternoon, with all the curtains open and my right hand in pole position. And when Michael B. Jordan struts shirtless onto the screen to challenge T'Challa for the throne of Wakanda, I am going to ejaculate with the ferocity of a heartbroken yet hopeful 12-year-old. I am going to nut all over the room, all over the pillowcases, all over the books I haven't read yet, the ceiling fan, my cousin's Glamourshot photo, my high school yearbooks, all over my mind's eye, and all over my memories of your glossy, naked paper-body. I'm going to do this with my real body. And my buckets of jizz.

This is not a good-bye, Antonio, and certainly not a promise to forget you. We humans will never be so simple as to choose that which remains in our memory, as much as we try to tell ourselves otherwise. But I am replacing you. Because, dimple-face, it is high time for me to brew some new mythologies.

And, for the record, Djimon Hounsou is way hotter.

THE WALK HOME

(after Julian Schnabel's *The Walk Home*)

I MAY BE WRONG, Dad, but I think that you think I don't think about you. I can sense it when you leave that rare message on my phone, as if I choose not to pick it up, and your voice goes tinny and far away: "Well, I'd like to hear how you're doing. I love you, son," with a lilt in your voice right at the end, an ellipsis, as if you think I would hesitate to say those words back to you.

What are you afraid of?

But I do think of you. Here's this: soon after the Broad Contemporary Art Museum opened on the campus of the Los Angeles County Museum of Art, Mark and I braved Wilshire Boulevard to see it, one of the biggest private collections in the world. I was teaching visual studies at a small art school at the time, and Mark and I had just moved into a converted 1924 MacArthur Park market building, a giant open space with polished concrete floors. We had a friend build out two bedrooms and, as a gift, he made for us a 14-foot-long wood plank table to accommodate guests for those rather large Sunday dinners I've told you I hosted for years. Mark was very excited about this place. He would say, "It's our first home together," and squeeze my hand. But I didn't tell you any of that, because, well, you wouldn't have wanted to hear it then.

On the second floor of the Broad, adjacent to the extensive Cindy Sherman and Jasper John collections, was a single large-scale Julian Schnabel, one of his broken plate paintings from the 80s, "The Walk Home." It is an abstract work on six wood panels, the suggestion of a stand of trees made of oil, copper, fiberglass and, of course, the iconic broken plates that signature-d Schnabel as an art-world sensation. I know you don't care about any of this, but my reader might, so I indulge. The part where you come in: I sat in front of this art work for a very long time, and thought of you, and cried, not in the way we mourn a loss, but in the way we realize a feeling we don't fully understand. Mark sat very beside me and held my hand. He didn't have to know why I was crying, and that should tell you why I love him.

There are all kinds of homes, Dad. Humans have lived in some unlikely shit! And I don't mean inside caves or among the branches of trees. I mean under*ground*, or on the sides of precipitous cliffs, tunnels in abandoned subways, storage spaces in Rhode Island shopping malls. And, igloos? An arch of ice as shelter?

You were hardly ever home, and ours was a classic, run-of-the-mill brick or wood or stucco thing that kept us warm. Mama made it as warm and safe as she could, but you were never there.

I always perceived you as a nice man, and you are. You're goofy, you crack terrific dad jokes, sing happy birthday so off-key you earn applause. You're well-liked by your co-workers, your neighbors, loved dearly by my younger sister and her mother, your second family.

But you weren't ready for your first, especially when fatherhood pounced on you at 20. And you ran, first just away, and then straight into the Marine Corps, and from there, I don't know where you went.

But when Mama ran from home, ironically into another Marine's arms, you were left with two kids—a seven-year-old me and an already wild-eyed and eruptive 14 year-old Chris. Man, you weren't ready for that. I believe you loved us, I really do, but you sucked royally at the parenting thing. I guess it was just too much to deal with. You were gone so often, you couldn't have called us by our true names. You didn't know what we liked eating, so you bought lots of pot pies. Stacks of pot pies. Pot pies, hot dogs and mustard. You didn't know that when I retreated to my room it was to read and speak to my imaginary older sister, and that Chris was already drinking booze and fingering girls behind the K-Bay store—the beginning paths to our becoming. And when you were re-assigned to Quantico, Virginia, it didn't seem like you wanted to know. You dropped us with your parents in Maryland and disappeared again. When you re-emerged, it was with a new wife, a new life. What then? What kind of home were you thinking to provide?

So, yes, on paper it was a military ranch-style house next to a cemetery, filled with new people: your new wife, Pamela, her son, Blair, and baby Bridgette. I guess we tried to make a home, we tried to get along, but you were never there. And don't say it was work. No Marine worked as late and as often as you. And Pamela didn't know what to do with us—one kid lonely and unmoored by the tumult, the other completely untethered and wild from losing his trust in the two people who mattered most—and she foundered, to put it diplomatically. Chris ran away, and I stayed outside to avoid the home I never felt welcome in, as late as I could. I hung out in the woods beyond the military housing complex.

It was in those woods that I was assaulted by one of the men that lived there. He was someone I recognized, someone you had a friendly face for. The stand of early spring trees, dead leaves decaying on the ground, the evening light between branches. Tall silhouettes patterned with dusk, plunging into the dirt. My face slack in the dirt. The smell of the dirt and my own body turned inside out. The making of mud with my own mouth. Pain and its taste of mud and metal.

I don't know if he knew I was your son. You didn't know about the assault. I told no one. I walked home, my shoes disappearing with my ever-slow pace into the darkening night, my body an upside-down "Y" to keep the pain smaller. The house was empty. I drank a glass of water and sat on the edge of my bed in the still air of the bedroom and watched the remaining light fade from the window. The next morning I left the house without speaking to anyone. It was easy to tell no one. I was afraid to, anyway. I was ten years old, and in some strange way I blamed it on what you referred to as my "sissy behavior."

Broken plates frame Schnabel's painting, jagged edges cutting into the thin tree trunks. Maybe Loblolly pine or eastern redbud. Thin, barren, without the coverage of spring.

Chris needed you, Dad. So did I, even though I have convinced myself over the years that I didn't.

That was why I needed to leave. Mama had recently moved to Maryland and, after one visit with her, I knew I still needed a home without knowing the word for it. She was now married to another man (the man you accused her of cheating on you with in Hawai'i), living in a trailer park outside of Baltimore, but the promise of it seemed better somehow.

I thought moving in with Mama was going to give me that home I needed, and it did in some ways. When I recall this period, I think of making eggs with her in the kitchen, I think of blender milk shakes and games of Yahtzee and Scrabble, the stuff of home. But her being married to this new man, a schizophrenic, alcoholic ex-Marine, it was a home primed to be blown down.

By the time I graduated high school, I had moved 13 times. You may know this, perhaps only as anecdote, and not for how you should know it.

After my first year of college in Atlanta, I decided not to return to Maryland, and instead rented a small cottage in the city with some friends. I had just come out of the closet and craved to build the rest of a home around it. That summer you lent me money to buy a used 1982 Chevy Malibu that I called Agnes Faye Chiquita. It was yellow, and the clock displayed a random assortment of numbers at any given moment (Agnes is a character in the play *The Shadow Box* whose senile mother repeatedly asks of her daughter, "What time is it, Agnes?" *The Shadow Box* was the very first drama I was cast in, but you wouldn't know that, because you didn't know I was a Theatre minor). I called to thank you. You told me you loved me but didn't approve of the "life I chose." I thanked you again, hung up the phone and wondered how you could know any of the choices I had made. I could count on my hands the numbers of times I had talked with you in ten years, and we never discussed anything as profound as choices.

The Christmas after your father died, I asked to see you. Remember that? It had been some years. I saw gray in the hair around your temples. Your father was notoriously grudge-holding, and some time before his death, he disowned your brother for, in my estimation, Sicilian nonsense. He died never having invited his son back into his life, and that detail was what made me feel so sad upon his death. I realized I did not want you dying without knowing your own. It was lightly snowing, and we were walking along the edge of Grandpop's property. You told me you wanted to be closer to me. You told me that you loved me. I believe that you did, Dad. But you also told me that you'd still like to discuss "this lifestyle I chose," as if consultation would lead to some virtuous purgation. I told you with a slit of a mouth there's nothing to discuss, that if you wanted to be in my life, you had to accept all of me, just as I had accepted all of you. Even then, I saw you see something in me. You looked at me different. Months later, you surprised me by attending my college graduation, and that was the beginning of something, something more than what we never had.

One late summer afternoon, years later, I was sitting on the squat porch of my decrepit yet entirely satisfying Hollywood cottage. The orange tree was overloaded with its oddly petroleum-tasting fruit, the small garden browning from our water-conservation efforts. My roommate, Irwan, was cooking yellow curry that sharpened the air for our weekly Sunday dinner where a couple dozen friends and neighbors came over with wine and weekly musings, and we shoved together picnic, dining and end tables into the driveway, our motley al fresco banquet. I heard the faint strumming of a guitar from my other roommate's room. And I felt this deep sense of belonging, like I was home, really home, perhaps for the first time. These sounds, these smells, the Sunday ritual. They were familiar, of family. I looked again at the orange tree, the garden. The moment was not long, nor underlined by dramatic thinking, yet became a resolute memory, something chosen. Weeks later, I met my husband Mark. I don't perceive this as coincidence.

I have lived in many kinds of houses. I've lived in turn-of-the-century clapboards, generic 70s dingbat flats, converted bank buildings, soaring ceiling lofts, trailers, skinny rowhouses. I currently live in a Victorian shotgun in the Western Addition of San Francisco. It is the longest I've ever lived in a single dwelling, a single place. Place. Where one is placed.

I wish you had created a home where I could have told you, Dad, a home where I wouldn't have entered an empty room that closed me up, where I wouldn't have sat alone on that bed with the dying light, where you would have pulled me tight and told me it was not my fault, would have walked me to the edge of the yard and stood with me in the stillness, would have silently plotted the revenge against your trespassing neighbor. Would have helped Chris and I adjust to your new family and helped them adjust to your old one. Would have been there. There are so many woulds in this passage. A stand of woulds, without the coverage of spring.

I'm not sure if this essay is for you, or me. Who is coming home? Where shall we walk? Is it wherever we walk that meets in the middle?

I talk to you fairly often now, more than I ever have. The conversation usually revolves around what school I'm teaching at, how your hand is feeling after the surgery, what movie Mark is working on. You love Mark, think it's so cool that he's a movie-man. You crack a few old dad jokes, and the goofy sincerity makes me laugh. You tell me every phone call that you are proud of me, that you love me. You are a nice man. Maybe even a good man.

I fly back to Maryland this summer to be with you for Father's Day. We drive to Ocean City—you, Pamela, Blair and his new wife, Bridgette and her family, and me—to watch the Blue Angels line and loop over the muddy Atlantic on a sunny day. We eat pizza and dig our toes in the sand, all facing the edge of the world, that awesome seam between water and air. The breeze is good. You say that you wish Chris were here, that he would talk to you, in that tinny and far-away voice. I give you a sympathetic pursing of my mouth, but say nothing and go back to the ocean.

I see the way Bridgette looks at you, your grandchildren, the way they will lay themselves on your shoulders. In this, I see that you learned to come home. You may not have been home for me, for Chris, but eventually, you found your way. And for this, I feel something good.

EYEWITNESS

THIS IS A FAVORITE. One of a few photos that I deem a keepsake. The laughter. Mama's red hair every which way, and a feeling familiar as a kitchen cabinet: easy to open and you know what's in there. Me all toothy and flesh, the joy so on the tops of our skin that not even Mama can hide her smile before the photo is taken. I can sink into this picture, my vision wholly encompassed within the frame, and I become the entirety, and then I assume the image's environment, the russet carpet, the eggshell walls, the cherry-wood lattice of the TV hutch, the baby Philodendron, shades of brown with a brooch of green. I watch my chunky limbs wiggle against the fabric of her jeans, and the photo takes on the vibration and sway of a fully-living world. I am rocking in her lap, her laugh making me laugh more, until the giggles cramp our sides.

What follows is just as vivid: we are now in the kitchen making chicken and dumplings from scratch, me dropping thumb-sized dough into hot oil on the stove. The Formica countertop is chipped and not quite white, not quite yellow. Mama picks me up. We scoop into the thick mix of flour and butter and water with the spoon. I drop another wet dollop, and watch it immediately bubble and brown. I am fascinated by the change, only knowing the physics of my own body and not even that, let alone the intricate properties of heat on other things.

How is it even possible that I remember this much detail? I was so young, 2 1/2 years old, maybe? Too young to remember this. Mama corroborates that we wouldn't have made dumplings that day, anyway—she didn't have a deep fryer in Camp Pendleton. Why do I have this particular memory, then? What inspires me to have it appear so resolute with each glance of this photo? Mama

reasons with a shrug that I probably just merged a moment that I do remember into this one.

Helene Intraub and Christopher Dickinson would perhaps argue that what I experienced is called boundary extension. The scientists claim that we report false memory beyond the boundaries of a view after less than 1/20th of a second. In their 2007-08 experiment, photographs of scenes were interrupted by a 42-millisecond mask on a multitude of viewing subjects before the scene reappeared. Post-interruption photographs that were unchanged were rated as closer up than the original views. The observers remembered pre-interruption views with extended boundaries. The brevity of these interruptions implies something about the way we visually scan for information and certainly how we then make it a file in our memory.

Sitting on a patio drinking beers with my bestie, Katie. I recall a choice picture I saw of her on Instagram in a wide smile at a New Years Atlanta house party. In my description of the beloved photo I include that her friend Jeremy was grinning next to her, his russet beard framing a very broad smile, something joyful. Katie pauses, slides her beer on the table in confusion, disclosing there's no way Jeremy was at that party, as he had journeyed to Wisconsin for a new life by then, and was way too broke from the fresh move to visit. I still myself, flummoxed, trying to imagine the photo—so clear and resolute in my memory—with Jeremy's gleaming face in the left edge of the frame. I was not in Atlanta for this party, having already moved to California by then. From where did this added memory emerge? And why was it so resolute in my recollection?

Intraub and Dickinson confirm the existence of false memory after an interruption briefer than an eyeblink. If that can occur within milliseconds, imagine how the boundary extension can be applied to years of memory recall, which essentially—akin to perception—is pulling up a visual file from our experience database accompanied by specific sensory detail. Like a Smell-O-Rama photograph, or a picture with a soundtrack. Perhaps the false memory discovery of Intraub's and Dickinson's experiments magnifies with time, with more possible information affecting that particular file in our minds. The extension of the boundary moves beyond the frame in so many ways.

Perhaps I associated Katie's friend Jeremy with this moment of time in Atlanta. Maybe I associated him with the house in which the party was held. Or perhaps I fused him with the general concept of the New Year holiday. He somehow became a specific piece of sensory information that I collapsed into the narrative of this particular party with Katie.

Remember when I saw an alien in the backyard of my Baltimore rowhouse? A similar process of that failing perception—light and shadow cast on the retina, a chemical, an electrical impulse, an open file—operates for memory as well. Memory is less like a video recording and more like a composite of nerve reports, a recollection that resembles a collage of the various senses— sound in one part of the brain, vision in another, and so on—all coming together to assemble something like a kaleidoscopic whole, a Dada composition without manifesto. Hypotheses based on previous experiences fill in the spaces between each fragment to complete the picture. You can imagine the problematic nature of such an action.

New Years/Atlanta/Katie? Jeremy. New Years/Atlanta/Katie? Jeremy. A chemical, an electrical impulse, a file, guesses filling the interstices. And then, a reality of some kind.

I have many recalled instances of making chicken and dumplings with Mama. Here's another, sometime in my high school years. While our auburn mops hovered over the hot stove, Mama told me that upon leaving my father, before she moved into that small garden apartment across K-Bay from our Marine Corps base duplex, she asked me whom I preferred to live with. She drove me to school that day so that she could present me with the choice. She said that I paused, looked out the passenger window for a few quiet seconds, and then chose my father. When she told me this, I soured my face in disbelief, and exclaimed, "No way." I didn't know my father very well as a young child. He was always gone. The memories of my early life were almost entirely of my mother. My mother and I were so close, as close as you can imagine. Just look at the photo of us. You can see. But Mama insisted, said that she had also been surprised by my decision. I stared blankly at the bubbling of the fryer, the hissing of oil the only sound. Was that possible? Would I have chosen to live with my father? More importantly, would I have chosen not to live with her?

Another aspect of boundary extension is how a single event in our experience history will duplicate and play itself as a reoccurrence in our memories, especially if it is recalled and shared over time as something that bears importance. We duplicate the perception as a measure of its magnanimity, extend its presence to signify value.

I'm reminiscing with my friend Candace about our party days in Atlanta, the many nights we stumbled from Nomenclature or MJQ to Eleven50 to boogie down with Bad Boy Bill, Mark Farina or Steve Lawler. She cocks her head and says, "All those times? Miah, we went to Eleven50 once. It was so expensive, and you thought it was too bougie. We only went that one time because Digweed was spinning." But when I think back to that time 20 years ago, I see myself walking into the former theatre-turned EDM club staple many, many times. I can almost see the different outfits I wore—silver pants, overalls, poly tops with plumed collars and plunging necks—sauntering into the club's majestic Vaudeville glamour. Yet Candace shakes her head. It is only through corroboration with others, like this, that I can glean my mind's own deception. A series of overlapping shadows cast on the cave wall from a single source, a rather powerful—and flickering—flame.

If we can incur boundary extension from our own translation from eyes to mind, imagine if we add to those memories further information that has been associated with the experience. Eyewitness memory can also be altered by information supplied after the event.

Elizabeth Loftus, a psychological scientist who studies false memory, discusses how easily suggested our memories become when narrative information is introduced. In one of Loftus' most well-known experiments, subjects viewed a film of a car accident. Afterwards they were asked to recall to their best estimate the speed of the cars prior to impact. Some of the subjects were asked "how fast were the cars going when they hit each other" while others were asked "how fast were the cars going when they smashed into each other."

Subjects would reply with a significantly faster speed when the word "smashed" was used in the question. Furthermore, when the subjects were questioned if they recalled seeing broken glass in the video, the ones who were asked with the word "smashed" in the question were more than twice as likely to report seeing broken glass in the video despite none actually being present.

Fair enough, right? We know the power of language, the role of rhetoric, to alter our perceptions—even memories of things. The velocity of *smashed* compared to *hit* makes sense, yes? A fist *hits* a face, a hammer *hits* a nail into a wooden stud. A falling body *smashes* into the pavement below. A plane *smashes* into a skyscraper. We summon all of the instances we have experienced with both words in our mind's database, and the associations evoke an information all their own, in this case a speed.

In another of Loftus' experiments, she went further and introduced entire traumatic memories to her subjects. As children they were lost in a shopping mall, only to be found by an elderly stranger. None of these subjects had actually experienced this trauma in "real" life, yet one third of them recalled such a memory when questioned after it was introduced. That memory was now a part of their childhood, and while it didn't happen, it was real to those subjects. Resolute.

Eyewitness memory can also be altered by merging past experiences with other ones, a layering of memories, like two photographic negatives laid over each other. Maybe this is what happened with the chicken and dumplings memory. Maybe that memory was, let's say, one year later, in a different house, in a different state (Virginia this time). Maybe I fused the two together because of a single sensory detail, like the length of Mama's hair grazing my cheek, or a brooch of green catching my eye as I dropped dumplings into the hot oil. A single bridge between times, forever connected in my mind.

And then desire. Oh, yes. If language, if story, if colluded experience all modify the real happening into a memory, then what of the driving need to decorate our history? What if we desire to shape our past as a way to realize our present, without even knowing what we do? Perhaps we yearn to erase a feeling, arrest a destiny, prune the complexity of our narrative into a more legible story, something more clearly understood?

Don't we desire our story to be legible, even if only for ourselves?

What we know for sure is this: memory is not a video recording that we play back. It is as fallible, as wondrous, as tangled, as perception. If any information becomes associated with the file that we have created and stored into our mind, the information will become a part of the memory, or at least modify it, however slightly. And then, there is the telling. Each time we share our memory, we reconstruct it by fusing other events, altering it with language, superimposing other memories with it, integrating our desires into the history, shaping the tale with what others tell us.

Among even the most pivotal memories of our lives, how much is real? How much is true?

When I reminisced to my mother about my Bowie-inspired shirt switch-a-roo for my second-grade class photo, where I stripped off the white button-up and replaced it with my electric blue and mesh sleeveless, my mother cocks her head and says, "You didn't wear a button-up that day. We chose the mesh shirt for your class photo outfit." This is certainly not what I remember, at all. So, whose memory is "correct"? Whose motivation for a false memory is more acute: my desire to be OG punk rock, or my mother's desire to be the cool mama?

Sometime after I graduated, and before my college friend Michael wound up dead in that DC hotel room, he called me to ask if I would ever love him. During this call, he divulged there was this once, while we were hanging out in my dorm room some years before, that I implied I could see myself loving him, someday, when the time was right. I don't recall this moment at all. Was that his boundary extension, a time when we were listening to records in my room, and while my eyes were closed to catch the feeling he played a story borne from desire, that extended beyond those doleful eyes and into the secure corners of his memory later? Or is this a failure of my own memory, an edited-out sequence to make my story more legible? When I assured Michael over the phone that I would never have said such a thing, was his long, audible sigh on the other end of the phone more than merely disappointment, as I had suspected, but anger that I was lying?

At that same college a handful of years before, the night I laid in bed with K, did he merely allow me to crash in his room after an exhaustive night's worth of postcolonial theory-talk? Did I simply fall asleep with the overwhelming and lingering wish to kiss him, or was it indeed this first night of passion that I summon so resolutely many years later? How much of desire has fueled my own boundary extensions? I have to ask this question, even if this dangling memory, and the others, feel so close to the vine.

And Shenandoah. For several years my imaginary sister. What sort of boundary extension was this? A boundary so blurred? No, a boundary so broken? A desire beyond the frame of reality so great that it became a whole new world? Can a boundary break when hit with a certain kind of pain? Perhaps the better word would be smashed.

And what about the choice Mama presented me with all those years ago, whether I wanted to live with her or my father? For years, and quite often, I would stare blankly and marvel over this decision. Did I in fact choose to live with my father, this man whom all my life felt like a blur of a person? I don't believe I did. Did Mama embed me with this memory of a choice made, or is this what she actually remembers? Is this her own boundary extension, perhaps summoned to alleviate her guilt? I don't know. I may never know. What I do know, however, is this: I now have a resolute memory of sitting in a car with her and of this question being asked to my seven-year-old self. I see myself looking out the passenger window, and the brief pause, and the answer.

And what about this book? Memoir. A book of memories. And, also, subsequently, a book about false memories. By merely writing this book am I altering history, changing the course of my memory, or even my family's? Art functions as institutional commemoration of our culture. How much of this particular artwork is modifying the real, of my own design?

Maybe the question of "real" is very different than the question of "truth." Perhaps I've been asking the wrong question all this time.

What I perceive, what I identify, what I remember, what I recollect, what truth I glean from this recollection…each becomes its own discrete category in the sphere of my experience in time. What a journey this is, for me, perhaps for everybody. Perhaps this is why I write what you are reading now. I am becoming aware of the intricate properties of heat on other things.

And the beloved photo above, its yellowing account of my youth. How do I ask it of its reality?

This is all that I know, dear reader: no matter what the reality, there is a truth to this memory: joy. Love. May I keep this? For my own sake? Keepsake.

Art is a lie that tells the truth. What is true? Love. In the photo? Love. In whatever happened before or after, whether dumplings or a walk in the park, or an evening bath, I remember love here. In all the photos, in the language of them. Beyond the frame. The love around me. The love I've felt. The love I've given. The love I've accepted. The love I've mishandled. The love I've learned from. My boundary extension. However the love has manifested, has emerged from my memory—my so erroneous memory—it is the reality now. It governs my current actions and my current choices. A memory is many things. Among them, it makes a mind. It makes a body that follows. It makes a truth all its own.

Shall we enter?

THE SHAPE OF GRATITUDE

MY BIG MOUTH. There are twelve other people huddled onto a wood platform surrounded by trees, holding their orange and purple flowers, smiling brightly. Mark wears his powder blue suit, I'm in a white vest and knickers. But the center of this photo is my mouth. While everyone smiles, I'm gaping wide. I could be laughing. I could be yelling. I could be surprised. Or, perhaps, I am all of these. Photographs make still, a life.

This is one of many portraits, mine and Mark's wedding, a four-day romp at a summer camp in California's gold country. The camp had a lake and Gypsy Falls, zip-lining and silks, a giant swing, a fire pit for forty. People stayed on site. We gave all the cabins names: Wild Horses, Pie Fight, Living Room Dance Party, Hooker and the Camptastics, winking names for the folks that slept inside. Mark wanted a big wedding. I wanted one outdoors. Mark wanted great food. I wanted funky music. We wanted each other. And everything else wanted for naught. We made a home for four days, for us all.

The dry sun is only beginning to drop behind the canopy, but the air crisps to goosebumps, and everyone moves out from the earlier safety of shade. They corral into the lodge, where drinks are poured and pounded. Parliament Funkadelic swishes all the butts, and within two verses the best wedding boogie down you ever did see. If I was in the lodge—which I am not, yet—at the sight of such joy and abandon, I would have cried for the third time that day. The first was during my vows. The second

was for my family.

Before the pictures, before the handfasting and the reading of Neruda and our dog Butters stealing the show, I scream and jig in delight when I discover Mama bedecked in knickers, vest and a carriage hat. The day before, learning of my own outfit, she went into tiny Nevada City on a mission with help from my high school girlfriend, Michelle, and made, hands-down, the serendipitous thrift store score of the century. To my cool white and gray, she was warm brown and russet. Michelle called us, "The Dapper Duo." My friend Candace said, "You all are sooo mirror images." Mama and I grin; we certainly reflect each other, but not in the way of a mirror.

The night before, the hired taco truck arrived three hours late. Dana and Sean were still hanging lights for the reception. Marie was dazzling the groom-bed with glitter and chocolate. Geetika was slyly decorating the altar with a handcrafted banner and flowers. Some folks were meeting each other for the first time. Others were hiking down to the waterfall or fucking in the woods. Most were drunk and hungry from a full day of liquor and play. Just before that hanger sparked mutiny, Liz takes her iPod and summons Sly and the Family Stone. And upon the first beats of the speaker, a throng of legs collect into the dirt and an impromptu dance party kicks up the dust. We were staved. We were saved.

At the reception dinner before the dance miracle in the lodge, the microphone was hogged by a herd of speeches. Maybe it was the purple light, maybe it was the booze or something more sheer, but decrees of bond and love spilled from dozens of mouths—mouths I've kissed, mouths I've tasted, ones I've watched for years shape sounds of sorrow, of seeking. And then, my father's. My father, a man holding so few of my memories, his absence a closer thing to a memory, at all.

But one memory, long ago. My grandfather had died and I returned home for Christmas. We were walking in the snow, just the two of us, a first in a decade. He said, "I want to be closer to you." I said, "Then you'll have to accept all of me." He said, "I can't do that."

Now, fifteen years later, and more absence, his mouth quivered. In a moment of sincerity that only discovery can yield, surprising even himself, my father blessed the union and said, "I was wrong. I have never seen a love so strong." My friends knew my history. The collective gasp pulled all of the wind out of the woods. Maybe that is why we danced with abandon after. Something had been set free.

I live in San Francisco. My people live in Seattle, Phoenix, Nashville, Chicago, Asheville and Atlanta, Boise and Baton Rouge, Pittsburg and Park City, Australia and Spain. Some places I've lived, some lived with them, some lives ago. If you held a ruler up and traced lines between all of these points, you would obliterate the map. There would be left no names, no roads, no state lines, no boundaries.

Before the California chill settled upon the air, before the dance party that rocked my heart like a giant swing, Mark and I ran late to our ceremony. I was preparing my vows, moments before, writing them on paper ripped out of my journal. Mark teased, but not because he was mad. Later, when I shared why we were late to the stewed reverie, I heard, "Oh, Miah, always last minute," or "Just like Miah to make an entrance." I smiled. Those were certainly accurate accounts of me. But not for this. I wanted my vows to be an expression of that moment. I wanted to take in all the love from these people who taught me, who held me close. These people who forgave me, who were patient and loyal. I wanted to share the shape of my gratitude, a mouth open wide. I wanted, more than anything, to be honest.

ACKNOWLEDGMENTS & GRATITUDE

The following essays have been previously featured in other publications:

"The Modern Prometheus, reprise": *Interim*
"Just One Day Out of Life" and "The Treachery": *COG*
"Life on Mars": *The Stardust Review*
"Denotation/Connotation (or The Relativity of Shit)": *The Atticus Review*
"A Miracle of Miracles": *The Forge*
"Latitudes": *The Los Angeles Press*
"To An Ex-Lover": *Hashtag Queer*
"The Perfect Moment": *Folsom Street Food Court*
"Leaving a Mark": *Chelsea Station*
"Make Sure to See the Exit Door": *Wasafiri*

"Denotation/Connotation (or The Relativity of Shit)" is the winner of *The Atticus Review* Nonfiction Prize.

"Trying to Shove Ourselves Back Together" was a finalist for the Steinberg Essay Prize.

"Make Sure to See the Exit Door" was shortlisted for the Wasafiri Life Writing Prize.

For Bryan and Seth at Sibling Rivalry, for having so much faith in this collection before it knew what it was. And for being so encouraging and kind.

For my generous friends and colleagues, for reading these essays in their motley beginnings (and/or motley ends): Kazim Ali, Dana Bean, Carson Beker, Sarah Broderick, Maxine Chernoff, Katrin Gibb, Bob Glück, Irwan Iskak, Pat Johnson, William Johnson, Douglas Kearney, Kevin Killian (we miss you), Chad Koch, Jennifer Lewis, Paul Lisicky, Juliana Delgado Lopera, Randall Mann, Monique Mero, Toni Mirosevich, Ari Moskowitz, Danny Thanh Nguyen, Ploi Pirapokin, Baruch Porras-Hernandez, DA Powell, Shobha Rao, Stephanie Sabo, Janet Sarbanes, Kendra Schynert, Christina Tesoro, Chanan Tigay, Tony Valenzuela, Matias Viegener, and Arisa White.

For my residency at Ragdale, where I began so many of these essays, and for the fellowship there with my fellow residents. And for Eula Biss and our after-dinner chats. You appear a few different ways in this book.

For my communities. My fabulous Foglifter fam. The love from folks at Nomadic, Lambda Literary, the CalArts crew, the Hub City gang, the writing program at San Francisco State, my Santa Clara University and San Francisco Art Institute colleagues. For the Bay Area's arms-open literary love. For Noah Sanders and the Racket series, for which I wrote the first of these essays. I feel supported from all sides.

For art.

For my chosen family. The best choice I've ever made.

For my biological family. This book could only be written with a deep love for you.

Mama, I know you'll feel it most, but it's the good kind of sting, the kind you know is working.

And for Marco. For being the best, for being so confident. I'm always burning up, burning up for your love.

ABOUT THE AUTHOR

Miah Jeffra is author of *The First Church of What's Happening* (Nomadic 2017), *The Violence Almanac* (Black Lawrence 2021), and co-editor, with Arisa White and Monique Mero, of the anthology *Home is Where You Queer Your Heart* (Foglifter 2020). Awards include the New Millennium Prize, the Sidney Lanier Fiction Prize, *The Atticus Review* Creative Nonfiction Prize, the Alice Judson Hayes Fellowship, Lambda Literary Fellowship for nonfiction, Hub City Writers Project Residency, and finalist for the Lambda Literary Award for Outstanding Literary Anthology. Miah is founding editor of queer literary collaborative, Foglifter Press.

ABOUT THE PRESS

Sibling Rivalry Press is an independent press based in Little Rock, Arkansas. It is a sponsored project of Fractured Atlas, a nonprofit arts service organization. Contributions to support the operations of Sibling Rivalry Press are tax-deductible to the extent permitted by law, and your donations will directly assist in the publication of work that disturbs and enraptures. To contribute to the publication of more books like this one, please visit our website and click *donate*.

Sibling Rivalry Press gratefully acknowledges the following donors, without whom this book would not be possible:

Anonymous (18)
Arkansas Arts Council
John Bateman
W. Stephen Breedlove
Dustin Brookshire
Sarah Browning
Billy Butler
Asher Carter
Don Cellini
Nicole Connolly
Jim Cory
Risa Denenberg
John Gaudin
In Memory of Karen Hayes
Gustavo Hernandez
Amy Holman
Jessica Jacobs & Nickole Brown
Paige James
Nahal Suzanne Jamir
Allison Joseph
Collin Kelley
Trevor Ketner

Andrea Lawlor
Anthony Lioi
Ed Madden & Bert Easter
Mitchell, Blackstock, Ivers & Sneddon, PLLC
Stephen Mitchell
National Endowment for the Arts
Stacy Pendergrast
Simon Randall
Paul Romero
Randi M. Romo
Carol Rosenfeld
Joseph Ross
In Memory of Bill Rous
Matthew Siegel
Alana Smoot
Katherine Sullivan
Tony Taylor
Leslie Taylor
Hugh Tipping
Guy Traiber
Mark Ward
Robert Wright